Retire With Jesus

Finding Purpose, Peace, and Joy In Your Golden Years with Christ by Your Side

Ben A. Collingstone

Disclaimer

Retire With Jesus is a work of spiritual encouragement and personal reflection. While some stories and examples may be inspired by real-life experiences, all names and identifying details have been changed to protect individuals' privacy. Any resemblance to actual persons, living or deceased, is purely coincidental.

This book is not intended to provide legal, financial, medical, or psychological advice. It reflects the author's personal views, faith journey, and interpretations of Scripture. Readers are encouraged to seek guidance from qualified professionals or clergy for decisions related to retirement, finances, health, or spiritual matters.

The author and publisher disclaim any liability arising directly or indirectly from the use or application of any information contained in this book.

Dedication

This book is dedicated to my family. The pillars of my personal iron triangle.

Courage, Faith, Love

Preface

Retirement is often painted as a season of rest and reward—a time to slow down, travel more, and enjoy the fruit of a lifetime of labor. But for many, it also brings unexpected questions: Who am I now that I'm no longer working? What purpose does my life hold in this next chapter? Am I still needed?

This book was born out of those questions.

As I stepped into my own golden years, I found that the world offered plenty of advice on money management and leisure activities—but very little on spiritual renewal or how to walk closely with Christ in this sacred stage of life. I began searching for a deeper kind of retirement. One rooted not in fading relevance, but in rising spiritual strength. Not in what was behind me, but in what God still had planned ahead.

Retire With Jesus is an invitation to rediscover purpose, peace, and joy—not by clinging to the past, but by walking forward in faith. Each chapter offers biblical encouragement, heartfelt reflections, and practical insights to help you align your retirement years with God's enduring promises.

This is not the end of your story. In fact, it might just be the most meaningful part yet.

May this book bless and guide you as you step into this new season—with Jesus by your side.

In Christ,
Ben A. Collingstone

A retired computer scientist and friend of Jesus

Retire With Jesus:
Finding Purpose, Peace, and Joy
in Your Golden Years
with Christ by Your Side

Introduction.. 12

Chapter 1 Embracing Retirement as a
Sacred Season................................... 19

From Career to Calling—Redefining Your
Identity in Christ.....................................20

Letting Go of the Workplace—Trusting
God with New Rhythms.......................... 24

"What Now, Lord?"—Discovering God's
Purpose for Your Golden Years............ 30

Surrendering Regret—Finding
Forgiveness and Fresh Starts After
Retirement.. 36

Overcoming the Fear of
Irrelevance—Seeing Your Value Through
God's Eyes.. 44

Welcoming Change—A Faithful
Response to Life's Transitions..............49

Chapter 2 Building a Spiritual Foundation
for Daily Living...56

Creating a Morning "Quiet Time"
Routine That Works for You..................56

Seated Prayer Walks—Adapting Spiritual
Habits for All Abilities...........................62

Scripture Journaling for
Seniors—Reflecting on God's Promises...
68

Audio Devotionals and
Technology—Staying Spiritually Fed at
Home..81

Divine Reading and New Ways to
Encounter God's Word...........................86

Chapter 3 Finding Purpose Beyond the
Workplace..93

Serving as a Prayer
Warrior—Interceding for Family and
Community...93

Small Acts, Big Ministry—Phone Calls,
Cards, and the Gift of Encouragement....
100

Volunteering with Limited
Energy—Matching Service to Your
Strengths...106

Mentoring the Next Generation—Sharing Your Faith Story..... 113

Leading or Joining a Senior Bible Study—Building Community...............119

Embracing "Encouragement Ministry"—Blessing Others from Home... 125

Chapter 4 Navigating Loneliness and Grief With Christ...................................... 131

Reaching Out When It's Hard—Practical Steps for Building New Friendships... 137

Facing Holidays and Anniversaries After Loss..142

Grieving with God—Honest Lament and Biblical Hope...........................147

The Ministry of Presence—Finding Healing in Fellowship........................... 153

Remembering Your Loved Ones—Creating Spiritual Legacies After Loss..159

Chapter 5 Faith Through Health Challenges. 168

Trusting God with Your Body—Aging, Illness, and Divine Purpose................. 168

Adapting Spiritual Practices for Limited Mobility or Memory..............................174

Asking for Help—Faithful Approaches to Accepting Support.................................. 179

Praying Through Pain—Finding Jesus in Physical Suffering.................................. 185

Hospital Rooms as Holy Ground—Witnessing in Medical Settings 192

Finding Community When Homebound—Staying Connected to the Body of Christ...197

Chapter 6 Overcoming Fear, Anxiety, and Spiritual Doubt.. 204

Trusting God with Financial and Security Concerns..210

Battling the Fear of Dependency—Seeing Weakness as a Place for God's Strength...................... 217

When Prayer Feels Empty—Navigating Spiritual Dry Spells................................224

Facing Doubt Without Shame—Biblical Stories for Troubled Hearts................229

Cultivating Blessed Assurance—Practices for Resting in God's Faithfulness................................. 234

Chapter 7 Strengthening Family Bonds...240

Grandparenting as Kingdom Work—Creative Faith-Building Ideas. 240

Blessings and Prayers for the Next Generation...............................247

Navigating Shifting Roles With Adult Children......................................252

Sharing Your Testimony—Storytelling as Spiritual Heritage.................................258

Building Family Devotional Traditions..... 264

"Passing the Baton"—Encouraging Faith in Moments of Transition....................271

Chapter 8 Living Each Day With Meaning, Joy, and Hope................................. 277

Embracing the Slow Pace—Sabbath Rest and Renewal...284

Finding Joy When Loved Ones Are Gone. 289

Prayer for Joy in the Midst of Grief.....295

Looking Forward—A Heavenly Perspective on Aging............................297

Small Celebrations—Marking Milestones with Gratitude... 302

Living as a Light—Everyday Acts of Hope in Your Golden Years............................308

Conclusion.. 316

References...325

Introduction

The first morning of my retirement, I woke up early. I didn't need to. The alarm clock was silent for the first time in years. I sat on the edge of the bed, unsure what to do next. For decades, my days had predictable patterns—meetings to attend, problems to solve, computers to repair, coffee to gulp on the way out the door. Now there was none of that. Only quiet. My hands, so used to typing lines of code, fidgeted with the blanket. I wondered how I'd fill the hours. I wondered who I was, now that my job was done.

In those first days, I wandered through the house, straightening already straight things. I read the news twice. I tried a new recipe and remembered why my wife usually cooks. I took long walks, but each step seemed to bring a new question. Who am I, now that I'm not a computer scientist? Does my life still matter? What's next? I brought my confusion to God in prayer. Sometimes, my prayers were gentle. Other times, they felt raw and desperate: "Lord, what am I supposed to do now?"

If you're reading this, maybe you know a bit of that uncertainty too. Maybe you've felt that strange emptiness when the busyness falls away. Maybe you've lost the sense of who you are without your work badge or office chair. You might worry about your health, your finances, or whether anyone needs you now. Perhaps you feel lonely, even though you're surrounded by people. Or maybe you grieve for loved ones or for the parts of yourself that seem to have slipped away. These aren't just my struggles. They are the quiet questions so many retirees carry.

My turning point came on a morning much like the first. I sat with my Bible and a cup of coffee, feeling more lost than found. That day, I sensed Jesus with me—not as a distant Savior, but as a gentle friend who understood. I realized retirement wasn't just an ending. It was a sacred invitation to walk with Him in new ways. My identity wasn't gone; it was shifting, getting rooted in something deeper than a job title. That realization changed everything. Retirement could be a season of discovery and joy, not just a slow fade into the background.

That's why I wrote this book. I want to walk alongside you as you enter, or continue, this chapter. "Retire With Jesus" is both a guide and a companion. It's not only for the good days, but also for the hard ones. I draw from Scripture, my own stories, and practical habits that have helped me. My hope is you'll find encouragement, fresh purpose, and reminders that you are never walking alone.

This book is different from others you may have read. It's not just about having enough money or keeping busy. We'll talk about the heart—the longings, fears, and hopes that come with growing older. We'll look at what Jesus says about worth, purpose, and peace. Every chapter blends biblical wisdom with real-life stories and practical steps. My goal is to speak to your soul, not just your schedule.

Here's what you can expect if you read on. You'll discover how to find new purpose, even in simple tasks. You'll learn how to grow your faith in daily, doable ways. We'll tackle the fear and loneliness that sometimes creeps in. I'll share how you can leave a spiritual legacy for those you love. And, most of all, we'll look for joy—deep, steady joy—in ordinary moments.

As for me, I'm just a fellow traveler. I spent years as a computer scientist, solving technical puzzles and chasing deadlines. Retirement surprised me. It forced me to search for meaning beyond work and to lean on my faith like never before. I'm not an expert on aging, but I know what it's like to wonder, to struggle, and to hope. Now, I spend my days learning, praying, tinkering, and walking with Jesus. I still ask questions. I still have hard days. But I've found that this season is full of hidden blessings.

I know your journey may look different from mine. Maybe you're thriving. Maybe you're struggling. Maybe you're somewhere in between. Wherever you are, I want you to feel seen and understood here. This book is for you—to encourage you, to offer practical tools, and to remind you that you are still called, still loved, and still needed.

Let me give you a quick roadmap. Each chapter tackles a real challenge or longing of retirement. We'll talk about letting go of the past, building a new routine, and finding rest in God's promises. We'll explore serving others, handling loss, and nurturing hope. Every chapter offers stories, scriptures, and simple ways to put faith into action. You'll also find prayers and questions to help you reflect and grow.

So here's my invitation. Let's walk this road together. Let's discover what it means to retire with Jesus—not just to stop working, but to start a new journey of faith. There's more ahead than you might think. There is purpose, peace, and joy waiting for us. Let's move forward, hand in hand with Christ, into a season of abundance, grace, and renewed calling. Welcome to your next chapter.

Chapter 1 Embracing Retirement as a Sacred Season

"They will still bear fruit in old age, they will stay fresh and green, proclaiming, 'The Lord is upright; he is my Rock.'"
— *Psalm 92:14–15 (NIV)*

I'll never forget the Sunday after my last day at work. At church, a friend cheerfully remarked, "You must be loving all this time off!" I nodded politely, but inside I felt empty. My house was too quiet, my calendar filled only with doctor appointments or the rare lunch. I felt invisible, as though I'd faded from the busy world I once belonged to. That first week, I'd reach for my work badge out of habit, before remembering it was tucked away in a drawer. The long-awaited freedom now left me feeling lost. It's odd, isn't it? For years, our identity is tied to our job title, and suddenly it's gone. If you've ever sat at your kitchen table, coffee in hand, asking God, "What now?"—know that I have sat there too.

From Career to Calling—Redefining Your Identity in Christ

Retirement often unsettles our sense of identity. So much of life has been structured around work schedules, tasks, and roles that give us purpose. When those vanish, it's normal to wonder who we are now. I remember gazing out the window, questioning if I had anything left to offer. That question—"Who am I now?"—can quietly loom, causing us to doubt our worth. Many others face this same uncertainty after stepping away from a long-held career. Our culture's fixation on achievement makes it easy to feel diminished when we step out of the workplace.

Yet the Bible is full of people who underwent profound identity shifts, especially later in life. Moses spent years as a shepherd before being called to lead Israel—well into his eighties. Anna the prophetess saw her most significant spiritual impact in her elder years after decades of faithfulness at the temple. These stories show us that God's calling never retires; it often grows as our circumstances change.

Scripture assures us that our value isn't found merely in what we do, but in who we are in Christ. Ephesians 2:10 reminds: "For we are God's handiwork, created in Christ Jesus to do good works, which God prepared in advance for us to do." God still has meaningful things for us—work that may look different now, but is just as significant. I've known retired teachers who found joy tutoring at church, and friends writing letters to missionaries. These aren't just pastimes; they're examples of how God breathes new purpose into our lives.

If post-career identity feels elusive, pause to reflect on your identity in Christ. Try journaling: list words or phrases that describe you beyond any job—beloved child of God, encourager, listener, prayer warrior, grandparent, friend. Then note spiritual gifts or strengths you've seen over the years: hospitality, patient listening, teaching, organizing. Consider: how might God use these now? Seeing your history on paper can reveal passions and gifts that suggest new opportunities.

It also helps to introduce yourself differently at church or in social situations. Rather than, "I used to be an engineer" or "I'm retired," try, "I love praying for others," or "I'm passionate about helping kids read." Framing your identity around faith rather than previous roles shapes both your perspective and how others see you. Remind yourself with scriptural affirmations: "Beloved child of God," "God's workmanship," "Chosen and dearly loved." These are truths that define you now and always.

Reflection Exercise: Who Am I in Christ?

Set aside ten minutes to reflect quietly with a notebook. Title your page "Who I Am in Christ." Make a list of roles, qualities, or gifts that have nothing to do with your old job title. Pray over your list, asking Jesus to reveal one new way He wants to use these gifts today.

Retirement isn't the end of your story—it's a refocusing of your identity on what lasts. You are cherished by God and called for meaningful works He has uniquely prepared for you.

Letting Go of the Workplace—Trusting God with New Rhythms

The first few weeks without a work schedule can feel like being dropped in the middle of a silent field, the usual hum of purpose replaced with unsettling stillness. My calendar, once crammed with meetings and deadlines, now held only blank squares. I found myself pacing the hallway, missing the rhythm of early alarms, hurried breakfasts, and even that traffic on the way to work. The house seemed bigger, echoing with questions I hadn't faced before. I remember sitting in my favorite chair, restless, unsure whether to start a project or just turn on the TV. In those moments, it wasn't just boredom—it was a sense of emptiness that crept in. The loss of daily structure stirs something deep; it makes you realize how much comfort routine provides, even when it wore you out before. I missed feeling needed. The phone didn't ring as often. My email inbox became a quiet place rather than a source of constant requests. This transition is not just about time; it's about feeling at home in your own life again.

Finding new rhythms after retirement does not mean simply filling hours with tasks for the sake of busyness. It's about shaping your days around what nourishes your spirit. I started small—setting aside time each morning for quiet prayer and reading scripture before breakfast. Some days, I'd listen to hymns while sipping coffee, letting the music settle my heart. Then I'd plan something that brought joy: a short walk, a phone call to a friend, or a crossword puzzle at the kitchen table. I learned to schedule rest just as intentionally as activity, allowing my mind space to wander and reflect. A sample day for me now might include a "Morning with Jesus" routine—fifteen minutes of scripture, followed by a handwritten note to someone from church, a stroll through the neighborhood, or working on a volunteer project from home. Afternoons often hold a book or time in the yard, while evenings are set aside for family calls or quiet gratitude prayers.

Building such routines takes time, and you may need to try different patterns until something fits. Some friends of mine gather weekly for prayer at church, while others have found purpose volunteering at food banks or reading stories to children at the library. One woman I know started mentoring young mothers through her church's outreach program; another gentleman spends an hour each day calling homebound members just to chat and pray with them. These aren't grand gestures but steady ways of giving that fill the "needed" gap many retirees feel. If you feel unsure about where to serve, begin by asking God in prayer to open your eyes to needs in your community or church. Sometimes opportunities appear in unexpected places—a bulletin board message, a neighbor's request, or even a nudge during worship.

Feeling useful does not always mean being busy. Sometimes God calls us into seasons of rest as much as service. The Bible teaches us about Sabbath—not just as a weekly commandment but as a posture of trust that God works even when we do not (see Genesis 2:2-3). I struggled at first to accept that quiet afternoons could be holy ground. But over time, I noticed peace growing in those slower hours—moments when I would sit on the porch with my Bible, watch clouds drift by, and sense God's presence more deeply than in any crowded boardroom.

I've heard from others who found unexpected renewal in these slower rhythms. One friend shared how she began each day with twenty minutes of stillness and meditation on God's promises, finding her anxiety about health and aging softened by this new practice. Another gentleman rekindled his love for painting, using afternoons to create cards he sent to family and shut-ins at church. These acts became their offering—a gentle ministry that blessed both them and those around them.

Daily Spiritual Rhythm Planner

Try sketching out your ideal day below. Include time for devotion, rest, connection, and service—even if these blocks are small at first.

Time	Activity
7:30–8:00am	Quiet prayer and scripture
8:00–9:00am	Breakfast and light chores
9:30–10:00am	Phone call or card writing
11:00–12:00	Volunteer project or walk
2:00–3:00pm	Reading or creative hobby
4:00–5:00pm	Rest or reflection

7:00–8:00pm   Family time or gratitude

Unstructured time can be sacred space—an invitation to listen for God's whisper or simply rest in His love. Whether you are active or still today, trust that God values both your presence and your peace.

"What Now, Lord?"—Discovering God's Purpose for Your Golden Years

"For I know the plans I have for you," declares the Lord, "plans to prosper you and not to harm you, plans to give you hope and a future."
— *Jeremiah 29:11 (NIV)*

After the retirement cake is eaten and the well-wishes fade, a strange quietness settles in. You wake up, no alarm clock blaring, and wonder what to do with the hours stretching ahead. The calendar looks empty except for the occasional doctor's visit or family birthday. Underneath it all, an ache may whisper, "What now, Lord?" Many seniors find themselves asking if God still has a plan for their lives, or if the most meaningful days are behind them. This uncertainty is not a sign of failure or weakness. In fact, it can be the spark for a new, deeper conversation with God. The question "What do I do now?" is less about filling time and more about opening space for something sacred. God often uses these pauses to get our attention and invite us into new possibilities.

Sitting in my living room after retirement, I remember feeling adrift. I prayed, sometimes with words, sometimes with sighs. I asked God if there was something more He wanted from me. It felt awkward at first—I was so used to praying about work stress or family needs. But after a while, my prayers changed. I began to ask, "Lord, show me where You're already at work. Open my eyes to the needs around me." If you find yourself unsure how to pray in this season, start simply: "God, what would You have me notice today? Use me in some way, big or small." Sometimes answers come quietly—a neighbor's request for help, a church bulletin that catches your eye, or a nudge to call someone who might be lonely.

One friend of mine spent the first year of retirement feeling lost until she noticed how many people in her church missed regular connection. She started a small card ministry, sending handwritten notes to folks who were sick or grieving. Another gentleman discovered joy leading a men's Bible study every Thursday morning at the diner down the street. Their stories didn't begin with grand visions. They started with simple prayers and a willingness to take one step at a time. Sometimes God's purpose arrives as an invitation rather than a command—a chance to use what you already love in a new way.

You might find it helpful to map out your skills, interests, and resources as a way of listening for God's call. Take out a sheet of paper and create three columns: "Skills," "Passions," and "Opportunities." In the first column, jot down things you're good at—listening, fixing things, cooking, gardening, encouraging others. In the second, name activities that give you energy or bring joy—maybe singing in the choir, working with children, or writing letters. In the third column, write down needs you've noticed in your church or neighborhood—volunteer requests in the bulletin, people needing rides to appointments, shut-ins who rarely get visitors. Where your lists overlap may point toward your next step.

Retirement opens windows for ministries that are less visible but just as vital as any pulpit or committee. The "ministry of presence" is one example—simply being available for conversation, listening without judgment, offering prayer when someone shares a burden. These quiet acts matter deeply; they are not less important because they happen in kitchens or over phone calls instead of on a stage. In my own experience, I've found that sitting beside a friend during chemo treatments or praying with a neighbor after loss carries as much spiritual weight as any sermon I ever heard.

The Bible speaks gently but clearly about purpose at every age. Psalm 92:12-15 pictures the righteous flourishing "like a palm tree," still bearing fruit in old age and staying fresh and green. Value does not diminish with passing years; it often grows deeper roots. Sometimes the most powerful work we do is invisible—praying quietly for our grandchildren each morning or encouraging someone who feels forgotten.

Church announcement boards or newsletters are goldmines for discovering where your gifts might fit. Your local community center may post needs you can meet—a food pantry seeking help, a literacy group looking for tutors, or a hospital recruiting volunteers to visit patients. If it feels overwhelming to jump into something new, start small. Offer to greet newcomers at church once a month or join a group that meets for coffee and prayer.

God's purpose for your golden years may be quieter but no less beautiful than before. If you feel unseen or wonder whether your contribution matters, remember that listening ears and gentle hands often do more good than we realize. The world measures success by numbers or titles; God counts faithfulness over fame. This season holds opportunities not for chasing what's lost but for noticing what's newly possible—one simple act of love at a time.

Surrendering Regret—Finding Forgiveness and Fresh Starts After Retirement

"Forget the former things; do not dwell on the past. See, I am doing a new

thing! Now it springs up—do you not perceive it?"
— *Isaiah 43:18–19 (NIV)*

As I look back on my life, there are moments I wish I could rewrite—words I shouldn't have said, opportunities I let pass, relationships I could've nurtured better. For years, regret clung to my heart like a shadow. But then I read Isaiah 43: "Forget the former things... I am doing a new thing."

Those words weren't just for the past—they were for me, right now. Retirement isn't just an ending; it's a new beginning. In God's mercy, we are not defined by what we didn't do, but by what He is still doing through us. Letting go of regret makes space for renewal. Today, I choose to walk forward—freed, forgiven, and full of purpose.

Regret can be a heavy companion in these later years. Old memories, mistakes, and "what-ifs" tend to surface when life slows down. Sometimes, late at night, an old argument or a missed chance replays in my mind. I think about words I wish I'd swallowed, moments I let slip by, bridges I never mended. Maybe you know that ache too—the one that comes with remembering an opportunity you missed, a relationship that broke, or a promise you didn't keep. Regret sneaks up not only over the big things but the small ones too: a day wasted in worry, a kindness withheld out of pride, a door left closed out of fear. Retirement gives us time to reflect, but sometimes this reflection turns into self-criticism. We start to believe we're defined by our errors or shortcomings. It's easy to focus on the past and wonder if we've wasted too much time to make things right.

God doesn't want us to be trapped by regret. The Bible is full of stories about people who stumbled and started again. King David made grave mistakes, yet Psalm 51 shows his raw plea for mercy: "Create in me a clean heart, O God, and renew a right spirit within me." God forgave David and continued to use him powerfully. Peter denied Jesus three times in His darkest hour, yet after the resurrection, Jesus gently restored Peter by asking three times, "Do you love me?" Peter's greatest failures became the backdrop for God's mercy and new beginnings. These stories remind us that regret does not have the final word—God's forgiveness does.

Confession is the doorway to freedom. When I finally put my regrets into words—naming them before God without excuses—I felt lighter. Scripture calls us to confession not as punishment but as a release. You might try praying something like: "Lord, You know all the ways I've fallen short—sins of action and inaction, reckless words and silent pride. I ask for Your forgiveness and the courage to let go." Receiving mercy means accepting that Christ's sacrifice covers even the wounds we inflict on ourselves or others. Sometimes it helps to write a letter to your younger self. Pour out your regrets on the page: apologize for mistakes, offer yourself compassion for what you didn't know then, and speak forgiveness over those old wounds. When finished, you might tear up the letter or set it aside as a symbol of release.

Marking a fresh start can shape our spirits in practical ways. Lighting a candle while praying for forgiveness can become a physical act of surrender—watching the flame flicker reminds us that God's love burns away shame. Some plant a seed in the garden as a sign of faith in new beginnings; every sprout is hope rising from buried places. These rituals aren't magic—they're simply ways to invite our hearts into what God has already promised: "If anyone is in Christ, they are a new creation; old things have passed away; behold, all things have become new."

Sometimes what lingers most is unfinished business with others. If there's someone whose forgiveness you need or whom you need to forgive, consider reaching out. It might be a note, a phone call, or even just a silent blessing if direct contact isn't possible. Words can heal even after years of silence. Begin gently: "I've been thinking about you and wanted to say I'm sorry for how things ended," or, "I miss our friendship and wish things had been different." Not every attempt at reconciliation will lead to restored relationships, but extending the olive branch brings peace with your own heart.

Still, there are some wounds that can't be mended this side of heaven—loved ones lost before apologies could be spoken, situations that cannot be undone. In those cases, rest in God's promise to restore what was broken. Joel 2:25 speaks to this: "I will restore to you the years that the locusts have eaten." God redeems time and softens even the deepest scars.

You are not your past mistakes or missed chances. You are God's beloved child, wrapped in mercy each morning. Where regret tries to claim your mind, let forgiveness move you forward. Each day offers new mercies—a fresh page for your story—no matter what has come before.

Overcoming the Fear of Irrelevance—Seeing Your Value Through God's Eyes

It's hard to put into words how quickly you can go from feeling central to everything, to feeling like you're fading into the wallpaper. I remember overhearing two younger folks at church planning an event and saying, "Let's get some new faces on this." I smiled, but inside I felt invisible. It was as if I'd become part of the furniture—present but unremarkable. I've heard similar stories from others. One friend confided, "My grandkids barely glance up from their phones when I visit." Another said, "Sometimes at Bible study, I feel more like a relic than a resource." These moments sting more than we care to admit. The sense of being overlooked or left out, whether by family, church, or society, can creep in quietly but cut deep. For some, that feeling starts when adult children make big decisions without asking for input. For others, it shows up at church when new ministries seek "fresh energy," as if wisdom or prayer don't count. The fear of irrelevance is real. It grows in the silence after a busy life slows down, and it flourishes when our contributions are unseen.

Yet, God's Word tells a radically different story about our worth. In 1 Corinthians 12, Paul paints a picture of the church as a living body. Each person—a hand, a foot, an ear, an eye—is vital. Paul insists that every part matters, especially those that seem less visible. "The parts of the body that seem weaker are indispensable," he writes. This isn't just a metaphor; it's a blueprint for community. You may no longer lead the charge, but your role remains irreplaceable. Age does not disqualify anyone from meaningful service. Anna and Simeon in the temple were both advanced in years, yet God chose them to recognize and affirm Jesus as Messiah. Their testimonies shaped Mary and Joseph's understanding of what God was doing. Anna's daily prayers and Simeon's patient faith were not side notes—they were central to God's unfolding plan.

There are roles in God's family only seniors can fill. No one else can pray for missionaries with the wisdom born of decades spent on their knees. A handwritten note to a grandchild carries a kind of blessing that text messages can't match. When you share your faith story with someone new to church, your words carry a weight textbooks never will. Long marriages, hard-earned patience, battles through illness—these aren't just memories; they're living testimonies for others navigating storms of their own. I know several men who have made it their "job" to pray daily for every child in the church directory. One woman writes birthday blessings to each member of her extended family, her notes saved in drawers and hearts alike. These unsung ministries ripple outward in ways we'll never fully see.

You might not get applause or public recognition for these quiet acts of love and service. Still, they matter deeply in God's eyes. Sometimes the smallest gesture—a phone call to someone who's lonely, sharing a Bible verse with a neighbor—becomes an answer to prayer for someone else. I've seen this time and again. A retired nurse in our congregation started calling homebound members every Thursday afternoon just to check in and pray with them. She told me, "I don't have the energy to serve like I used to, but I can still be present." Those calls became lifelines for people feeling forgotten.

If you struggle to recognize your own value in this season, take time to notice your "unseen" acts of service. Keep a small journal and jot down each time you pray for someone, encourage a friend, or offer quiet support. Ask yourself: Who is blessed because I am still here? What have I given—love, time, wisdom—that no one else could? You may be surprised at how long your list becomes over just a few weeks.

Reflection Questions for Celebrating Unseen Value

- When was the last time someone thanked you for something small?
- What gifts or strengths do friends or family mention about you?
- How have you encouraged or comforted someone recently?

Consider reaching out to another retiree this week with an encouraging word. A note left on a neighbor's porch or a call to someone rarely seen at church can remind both of you that significance isn't measured by busyness but by presence and love shared.

God's economy looks nothing like the world's: quiet faithfulness counts for more than public achievement. Your worth isn't found in how loudly you shout or how many people notice; it's grounded in being seen and known by God Himself—and there is nothing irrelevant about that.

Welcoming Change—A Faithful Response to Life's Transitions

Change rarely asks permission before stepping in. Whether we're ready or not, new chapters arrive—downsizing into a smaller place, saying goodbye to a spouse, managing a new diagnosis, or shifting from the center of family gatherings to the edge. For me, sorting through old boxes in the attic before a move was bittersweet. Each photograph and forgotten trinket tugged at memories of laughter, loss, and everything between. Change brings both excitement and sorrow—a strange mix, like holding hope in one hand and grief in the other. You might look forward to freedom or a fresh start, but still feel the ache of what's ending. This tension is normal. In fact, it's human.

Transitions in these years aren't just about moving furniture or adjusting pillboxes. They can shake your sense of home, safety, and belonging. The first night after moving out of the family house, I lay awake listening to new creaks and unfamiliar silence, missing the chorus of familiar sounds. After losing my spouse, I found the empty chair at the dinner table louder than any conversation. Health changes mean letting go of certain routines or hobbies you once loved—golf replaced by gentle walks, baking swapped for store-bought bread. And when family roles change—children becoming caretakers, grandchildren growing up—the shift can leave you wondering where you fit now.

The Bible doesn't shy away from stories of change. Abraham's call came late in life, asking him to leave everything known for a new land, guided by nothing but faith and a promise. He didn't have all the answers, but he moved forward with God anyway. Naomi's story in the book of Ruth is another example. She faced devastating loss—her husband and sons gone—and returned to Bethlehem feeling empty and bitter. Yet from her pain came unexpected renewal as Ruth became both family and blessing. These stories echo our own: fear and loss walking side by side with hope and new beginnings.

Faith doesn't erase the sting of change but gives us tools to meet it with courage. I've learned to pray honestly in times of transition: "Lord, help me be brave enough to let go and open enough to receive what's next." Short prayers can carry tremendous strength when words run out. Sometimes I write down my worries or hopes in a journal, giving shape to swirling thoughts. Other times, I create small rituals—a simple blessing over a new home, a candle lit on anniversaries of loss, or planting a flower in memory of what has passed. These acts help mark endings and beginnings, giving space for both tears and gratitude.

Looking back, some of my hardest changes brought gifts I never expected.

Downsizing forced me to let go of clutter but made room for deeper conversations with family as we sorted through old stories together. After my wife's passing, friends from church showed up with casseroles, but also with quiet presence and understanding—companionship that eased the sharp edges of grief. A health scare led me to join a support group at church where I met people who prayed with me through scary test results and celebrated each small step forward.

God often leaves fingerprints on our transitions—signs that He is near even when the landscape shifts. Maybe it's a neighbor who becomes a close friend after you move, or a new hobby discovered because you had to slow down. Perhaps it's a sense of peace that surprises you after months of anxiety. If you pause to reflect, you may notice these unexpected blessings scattered like breadcrumbs along your path.

Reflective Prompt: Noticing God's Presence in Change

Think about a recent transition—big or small. Take a few minutes to jot down what was lost and what was gained. Where did you sense God's presence? Was there an unexpected kindness or new opportunity? Sometimes these moments are quiet—a scripture that comforts, a phone call at just the right time, laughter in the midst of tears.

Change will come again, sometimes gentle, sometimes fierce. When it does, remember you're not facing it alone. Faith doesn't guarantee that every transition will be easy or painless, but it anchors us in the truth that God walks with us through every unknown. In both the letting go and the starting over, His love remains steady—a promise that nothing is wasted and each season can hold beauty of its own.

Chapter 2 Building a Spiritual Foundation for Daily Living

"Therefore everyone who hears these words of mine and puts them into practice is like a wise man who built his house on the rock."
— *Matthew 7:24 (NIV)*

Creating a Morning "Quiet Time" Routine That Works for You

I used to wake up feeling lost, staring at the clock and debating whether to start the day or retreat under the covers. The quiet of the morning, while peaceful, could easily become a landscape for worries and aches to grow. Yet amidst that silence was a subtle pull—a chance to begin my day with God rather than old habits or the barrage of morning headlines.

In this season of slower mornings and fewer deadlines, I've found myself craving more than just rest—I've longed for rhythm. Not just routine, but a rhythm rooted in something deeper. Jesus reminds us that when we build our lives on His Word, we become like the wise builder whose house stands firm.

Retirement is the perfect time to reinforce that spiritual foundation—not just on Sundays, but in the quiet moments of everyday living. Whether it's morning prayer, Scripture journaling, or a simple walk with God in nature, these daily habits don't just fill time—they anchor the soul. The storms may come, but when the foundation is strong, peace remains.

Starting the day anchored in quiet time with God isn't about rigid rituals; it's about carving out a simple, intentional space to breathe, reflect, and remember who holds your future. Whether you rise at dawn or shuffle out late, what matters is setting aside a moment—however brief or unstructured—for God to center your heart. Bringing faith into the beginning of my day doesn't erase concerns, but it does help shrink them, granting me a more peaceful perspective.

A morning devotional can feel restorative. My friend Alan, never one for routines, started reading a Psalm over coffee for two weeks and described it as "tuning my heart before the world starts making noise." Another friend, Gloria, spent just five minutes in prayer and worship each morning; she found her anxiety eased and her patience with her grandkids increased.

These are not magic fixes, but even such small spiritual habits can bring calm and direction.

A quiet time routine works best when tailored to your real life. Many mornings are full of caregiving or appointments for some, while others enjoy leisurely starts. Keep your routine flexible—perhaps a five-minute devotion at the kitchen table (reading a scripture, praying, and quietly reflecting), or a half-hour of Bible study and journaling if time allows. Pairing prayer with your morning coffee can become a grounding ritual, letting the familiar aroma remind you of God's new mercies.

Caretaking duties or time with grandchildren may mean your quiet time looks different; keep it simple. Read scripture aloud while making breakfast or include young ones in a short prayer. Sometimes, my moment of reflection comes while folding laundry, using the task as a prompt to offer thanks for family. The key is intention, not getting it "perfect."

Distractions—whether sleepiness, electronic interruptions, or swirling worries—are normal. Preparing a "quiet time corner" the night before helps: set out your Bible, glasses, and devotional where you can easily reach them in the morning. A comfortable seat by a window or with a cozy blanket can anchor you. If you're prone to drifting off or starting chores mid-devotional, set a timer or quietly play soothing music to help focus.

A dedicated "quiet time corner" can become sacred: a favorite chair, a table for your devotional and coffee, maybe a candle or small plant—whatever brings peace and comfort. This doesn't require perfection but simply presence—a welcoming space to pause and connect with God.

Try This: Designing Your Own Quiet Time Corner

- Choose a quiet, comfortable spot.
- Keep your Bible and devotional handy.
- Add a calming element: plant, photo, candle, or mug.
- Set up your area before bed so it's ready for you.
- Pair your quiet time with another morning routine—such as your first cup of coffee.

Personalizing your quiet time routine makes it more meaningful and easier to maintain. Some pray with soft hymns in the background, others doodle in a journal or read scripture near an open window to listen for birds. One retiree even paints with watercolors while meditating on God's promises. There are devotionals created specifically for seniors, often with large print and relatable stories and prayers.

Remember, your quiet time can look however you need it to—it's about coming as you are, tired or awake, distracted or focused, and dedicating those moments to God. Over time, these simple, consistent habits bring a peace and guidance that can shape the whole day.

Seated Prayer Walks—Adapting Spiritual Habits for All Abilities

There was a time when prayer walks meant strolling through the neighborhood, greeting neighbors, and quietly blessing each house I passed. That changed when my knees began complaining and long walks became more of a memory than a reality. At first, I worried this meant my prayer life would shrink. But I soon realized you don't need to step outside to "walk" with God through the needs of your world. Prayer is not limited by your mobility, energy, or the number of steps you can take. Whether you're in your favorite armchair, sitting on the porch, or lying in bed, you can move through the landscape of prayer just as meaningfully. Seated prayer walks let you travel far, even if your feet never leave the floor.

Praying for others and for your community from a chair can be surprisingly powerful. There's something sacred about focusing your thoughts and petitions while gazing out the window, watching the morning light stretch across the yard, or simply holding a photograph in your hands. You might start with a mental "route"—imagine blessing each family member as you scan their pictures on the wall, pausing to lift up each face in prayer. Or perhaps you keep the church directory nearby and thumb through it, praying for members alphabetically or as names catch your eye. Some days, I set a world map on my lap and pray for faraway places—missionaries I know by name, countries in the headlines, or even towns where old friends live. Each place becomes a stop; each person, a holy appointment.

Setting up a routine for this kind of prayer looks a bit different than lacing up your shoes and heading outside. Gather what you need within reach—a basket of family photos, a directory, or even your smartphone with saved images. If you prefer structure, jot down a "prayer route" on an index card: start with children and grandchildren, move to neighbors or friends from church, then finish with global needs picked from the news or a mission newsletter. For world-focused praying, trace your finger along a map or use colored pins to remember places you've prayed over. Some folks clip newspaper headlines onto a bulletin board and pray through them each week, letting current events guide their petitions.

I've learned from others who have found deep meaning in this practice. Margaret, who once led women's Bible studies but now rarely leaves home, lines up framed photos of her grandchildren on her coffee table every Monday morning. As she sips her tea, she prays over each child by name—sometimes whispering specific requests, sometimes just asking God's blessing on their day. She says this habit has helped her feel connected even when distance or health keeps her apart from family. Another friend, Tom, subscribes to missionary newsletters and keeps them in a folder by his chair. He spends one afternoon each week reading updates and interceding for those serving overseas, feeling his prayers link him to God's work far beyond his living room walls.

Inviting others into seated prayer walks can turn a solitary practice into a community event. You might call a friend and pray together over the phone using the church directory as your guide. Some retirees form small groups that meet weekly—each person brings photos or lists of loved ones and prays aloud in turn. If technology feels comfortable, try setting up an online group chat where members share prayer needs and agree to "walk" through them at a set time each day. This can create accountability but also fosters companionship; you begin to look forward to hearing from others and sharing answered prayers.

Hosting a group seated prayer walk is simpler than it sounds. Invite friends to bring pictures or names they want to lift up. Light a candle as a sign of God's presence. Move through your lists together—pausing as people feel led to pray out loud or in silence. Some groups end by singing a favorite hymn or sharing how God has answered prayers since the last meeting. The connections formed during these times are often just as meaningful as the prayers themselves.

Sharing requests doesn't need to be complicated. Jot down names in a notebook and call someone once a week to see how you can pray for them. If you're more comfortable with technology, create a small text group for sharing updates and encouragements. Even mailing cards with written prayers can bless others immensely—especially those who might also be feeling isolated.

Seated prayer walks remind us that our influence is not measured by physical ability but by faithfulness and heart. There is dignity and purpose in this practice; praying intentionally for others each day brings hope not only to those you pray for but also to your own spirit. Even when your world seems smaller, your prayers can touch lives near and far. Every whispered blessing, every photo lifted in prayer, every map traced with longing—these are steps of faith that truly matter.

Scripture Journaling for Seniors—Reflecting on God's Promises

"For no matter how many promises God has made, they are 'Yes' in Christ. And

so through him the 'Amen' is spoken by us to the glory of God."
— *2 Corinthians 1:20 (NIV)*

As I look back over the decades, I see a trail of promises kept—some answered in ways I expected, others in ways I never imagined. There were seasons when I wondered if God had forgotten me, but in time, I saw His faithfulness unfold.

This verse reminds me that God's promises aren't vague hopes—they are guaranteed in Christ. Every "yes" He has spoken is still true today. Retirement offers the gift of reflection—time to pause and remember His goodness, to celebrate how far He's brought me, and to rest in the promises yet to come. When I whisper "Amen," it's not just agreement—it's gratitude.

There's a certain comfort in writing things down, especially when the mind feels cluttered or the heart feels heavy. Scripture journaling has become a lifeline for me in retirement—a gentle, steady way to anchor my thoughts and remind myself of God's faithfulness. It isn't about fancy words or perfect penmanship. It's about setting aside space to read a passage and let it soak in, then jotting down what stands out or what God seems to be saying in the quiet. When I write out a verse in my own hand, I notice details I would have skipped if I'd only read it silently. The act of writing slows me down, helping me comprehend and actually remember what I've read. Over time, these written verses become like stepping stones across a stream—each one helping me cross over doubts or worries that would otherwise sweep me away.

Journaling brings more than sharper memory; it brings healing. There have been days I felt anxious or ached with regret, and putting those feelings next to God's promises helped me see them with new eyes. Sometimes, in the simple act of writing, tears come. That's not weakness—it's release. Being honest on the page has helped me process grief, celebrate small victories, or spot patterns of God's provision through the ups and downs of aging. There's something powerful about seeing your own handwriting next to the timeless words of scripture—a living conversation between you and the Lord.

If your hands tremble or your eyes strain over small print, don't let that stop you. I switched to a large-print journal and thick, easy-grip pens after my arthritis flared up. Some friends use spiral notebooks and write big, leaving plenty of space between lines. Others dictate their thoughts into a phone or tablet using voice-to-text apps. If screens work better for you than paper, audio journaling can be just as meaningful—record your reflections and listen back later, or even share them with family. The format isn't sacred—the practice is.

Starting can feel awkward, so I keep it simple. I pick a short passage—maybe two or three verses—and write them out at the top of the page. Then I ask myself: What stands out? How does this connect with what I'm feeling today? If my mind goes blank, I use prompts tailored for this season of life. One that always opens my heart is, "How has God been faithful in my life?" Another: "What promise of God speaks to my season?" Sometimes I write about a specific worry and then find a verse that addresses it, finishing with, "What is one worry I can surrender today?" These prompts aren't rules—they're invitations to start a real conversation with God on paper.

To make this habit stick, I create little rituals around it. Sometimes I light a candle before I begin, or play soft music in the background. My journal isn't fancy; pages are dog-eared and scribbles run off the lines. Some days I only manage a sentence or two, others I fill several pages. It's not about how much you write but showing up honestly.

Sharing these journal entries can multiply their meaning. On quiet afternoons, I've sat with my granddaughter and read her an entry about how God helped me through a tough time years ago. She listened wide-eyed—and later said it helped her pray about her own fears at school. Passing along our written prayers or reflections to loved ones can become a legacy—a spiritual heirloom for children and grandchildren who may one day wonder how faith shaped us.

Some have started what they call a "legacy journal." In these pages, they collect not just scripture notes but stories from childhood, prayers for each family member, blessings for future generations, and hard-won wisdom from years with the Lord. You don't need to be eloquent—just honest and willing to share how faith has mattered through both sunshine and storms.

For those who prefer structure, here's a template that's worked well for me:

1. Write out a verse or two that speaks to you today.
2. List one way you've seen God's faithfulness in your life—recently or long ago.

3. Reflect on a promise from scripture that gives comfort or strength.
4. Name one worry or regret you want to surrender, then write a short prayer giving it to God.
5. Finish with a blessing—for yourself or someone you love.

No two journals look alike because no two lives are the same. What matters most is not filling pages but building trust that God's word is active in your day-to-day life—even when days feel ordinary or uncertain. Each entry becomes a small altar of remembrance, marking where God met you right where you were.

Gratitude Lists—Finding Joy in Everyday Blessings

I didn't always pay attention to small blessings. There were stretches when my thoughts clung to what was missing, aches in my body, or the news on TV. But I found that something changed inside me when I started writing down what I was thankful for. Science backs this up—the brain actually forms new pathways when you practice gratitude, making it easier to spot the good, even on tough days. Researchers say it helps with sleep and mood, and even staves off loneliness and depression. The Bible echoes this wisdom. Paul wrote letters of thankfulness from prison, counting blessings when he had almost nothing but faith and hope to his name. In 1 Thessalonians, he urges, "Give thanks in all circumstances." Paul's words ring differently when you know his story—he was in chains, yet he still found reasons to thank God.

Keeping a gratitude list isn't complicated. Some folks keep a small notebook by their favorite chair or on the bedside table, jotting down three things each night before bed. Others use a gratitude jar: write a brief note about a moment you appreciated—a smile from a neighbor, the taste of fresh peaches, a hymn on the radio—and drop it in. Over time, these notes create a record of God's faithfulness you can pull out and read on days when joy feels out of reach. I've met couples who share a gratitude calendar on the fridge, each taking turns adding to it before breakfast. More than once, my wife and I have challenged each other to name something new every day for a month—no repeats allowed! Inviting someone else makes the practice more fun and keeps you honest.

There are plenty of ways to keep the habit fresh. Some days it's easy to write "family," "health," or "home," but looking for less obvious gifts trains your eyes and heart. Thank God for the scent of old hymnals, the way sunlight glints off your coffee cup, or the first daffodil of spring peeking through last year's leaves. On rainy afternoons, I've written down gratitude for memories—like an old friend's laughter or a story my dad used to tell. Sometimes I notice God's goodness in routines: folding warm laundry, hearing birds chattering before dawn, or finding my keys on the first try. There's even joy in things that used to annoy me—like the clatter of the mail slot or the creak of floorboards—because they remind me this house is still full of daily life.

When discouragement settles in or loneliness lingers, gratitude can be a sturdy anchor. On my hardest days, I've forced myself to write thank-you notes or encouragement cards to others. There's something about turning outward that lifts the spirit; seeing someone else's face light up from an unexpected note is its own reward. At church gatherings or Bible studies, sharing what we've written can transform the mood of a group—one person's gratitude sparks another's memory of a blessing. Sometimes we pass around a basket and read our notes aloud. These moments remind us that none of us is ever completely alone in what we're feeling.

Visual Exercise: Your Personal Gratitude Jar

Find any jar—mason, peanut butter, pickle—and place it somewhere you'll see daily. Each morning or night, scribble one thing you're grateful for on a slip of paper and add it to the jar. When you hit a rough patch, reach in and read several at random. Watch as your collection grows; it becomes proof that God is present in ordinary things.

Mixing up your prompts can help keep your list lively throughout the seasons. In spring, thank God for new blooms and longer daylight; in summer, for cool breezes or backyard gatherings; autumn brings colored leaves and warm drinks; winter may offer cozy blankets, Christmas cards, or memories from years past. You might focus on people one week—neighbors who wave from their porch, church friends who pray for you—or recall favorite hymns and scriptures that have comforted you through loss.

Gratitude lists aren't about pretending everything is perfect or ignoring pain. They're about looking deeper—naming God's faithfulness right alongside life's messiness. Each entry is an act of faith: I see you, Lord, even here. Over time, these simple lists become more than words—they become quiet testimonies that shape how we see ourselves, our days, and our future with hope.

Audio Devotionals and Technology—Staying Spiritually Fed at Home

There are days when flipping through a printed devotional feels like too much effort, or my eyes blur over the words after a few minutes. Sometimes, it's just easier to listen. Thankfully, there's a whole world of spiritual resources you can hear rather than read, right in your own living room. If you have a smart speaker—maybe an Alexa or Google Home—you can ask it to play the Daily Hope devotional or a favorite Christian radio station. I admit, the first time I tried it, I felt a bit silly talking to a machine, but now it's second nature. You can say, "Alexa, play Bible verses for today," and she'll start reading scripture out loud. Apps like YouVersion offer audio Bibles and daily devotions, and they're free. Even if you don't consider yourself "techy," these tools are designed to be simple. Just download the app to your phone or tablet, tap "devotional," and choose what fits your mood that morning.

Some friends of mine prefer Christian podcasts. There are plenty aimed at seniors with gentle voices and real stories about living out faith in retirement. "Guideposts" has an audio devotional for older adults, and "5-Minutes and a Coffee" gives quick encouragement that fits perfectly with your first cup of joe. Ministries like "Daily Hope" or "Abide" speak directly to those facing the transitions of aging, focusing on hope in God's promises when life changes faster than we expect. If you're interested in learning more about scripture, "Ask Pastor John" answers tricky questions in plain language, and "By Faith" brings in guests who discuss real-life faith challenges, illness, and even grief with compassion. These podcasts help keep faith fresh even when you're at home alone, and you can pause or rewind if you want to hear something again.

For anyone who feels nervous around new technology, or if typing on small screens is tough, there are workarounds. Ask a family member or a tech-savvy friend to help set up the device or download apps for you. Adult children often like being asked for tech help—it gives them a way to care for you that feels practical and loving. If smart speakers seem intimidating, try starting with something as simple as a phone-in prayer line. Many churches and ministries offer daily devotions you can hear by calling a toll-free number. Even if eyesight fails or fingers fumble with small buttons, your telephone can be a lifeline for spiritual encouragement.

For those with vision impairment, many audio devotionals come with adjustable speeds and volume controls. Closed captioning on smart TVs can make understanding easier if hearing is an issue. Some audio Bibles are available on CD or MP3 player—no internet needed—so you can listen with just the push of a button. Don't hesitate to ask someone at church about their favorite resources or for help setting up a device; folks are usually eager to share what's worked for them.

Listening doesn't have to be solitary. Some of my favorite mornings involve a "devotional call" with friends. We'll all press play on the same podcast or devotional at the same time—sometimes over the phone, sometimes just knowing we're each listening at home—and then chat about it afterward. It's a gentle way to stay connected when getting together isn't possible. If you'd rather meet as a group, try starting a Zoom Bible study for retirees. The technology might take a bit of practice at first, but after a few calls, it feels natural. The conversations that follow often go deeper than small talk; we end up praying for each other's families and laughing about the things only fellow seniors truly understand.

If you're feeling isolated or want to try something new, consider inviting another retiree—or even your grandchild—to join in listening together from afar. Sharing your thoughts afterward builds connection and helps keep faith conversations alive across distance and generations. You might even discover that your willingness to try new things inspires someone else to do the same, opening up fresh ways for both of you to grow closer to God without ever leaving your favorite chair.

Divine Reading and New Ways to Encounter God's Word

"Your word is a lamp for my feet, a light on my path."
— *Psalm 119:105 (NIV)*

For years, I saw Bible reading as a task—something I "should" do, like taking spiritual vitamins. But in this slower, sacred season of life, I've discovered something deeper: God's Word is alive, personal, and surprisingly fresh.

Psalm 119:105 reminds me that Scripture isn't just for the past; it's a lamp for the path I'm still walking. Now, I approach it differently—not rushing, but lingering. Sometimes I journal, sometimes I sit in silence after a verse, letting it speak. God's Word meets me where I am, lighting the way, one promise at a time.

There are times reading the Bible can feel routine, like you're just skimming words without them reaching your heart. I found myself in that place after retirement, flipping through familiar passages but feeling disconnected. Then I discovered Divine Reading, a gentle approach that made scripture feel fresh again. The phrase means "sacred reading," and it's not complicated or mystical. It's simply a way to slow down, listen, and let God's voice come through in a more personal way. You don't need a theology degree or special training. All it takes is a willingness to linger with the Word.

Divine Reading is built on four simple steps anyone can try. First, you read a short passage—just a few verses, not a whole chapter. Read slowly and out loud if you can. Next comes reflection: sit with the words and notice what catches your attention. Maybe it's a phrase or an image, or even something that puzzles you. Third, respond. This might be a short prayer, a question for God, or a feeling you speak aloud. Finally, rest. This is a quiet moment to just be with God, without any agenda—much like sitting with an old friend in comfortable silence. For beginners, I'd suggest picking accessible verses from the Psalms or the Gospels. Psalm 23, John 14, or Matthew 11:28-30 work beautifully because their language is simple and their themes—comfort, hope, rest—speak to our stage of life.

Scripture comes alive in new ways when we use more than just our eyes and ears. One approach I enjoy is listening to dramatized Bible readings—stories told with music and different voices that help me picture the scenes more vividly. Even on days when my focus is scattered, hearing scripture read out loud pulls me in and lets the words settle differently than silent reading ever did. Some friends have tried "coloring scripture"—using colored pencils to highlight words or sketch simple pictures in the margins as they listen or read. Don't worry about artistic skill; the point is to engage your heart and mind in ways that feel right for you. Bible art journaling can be as simple as drawing a cross beside a verse that comforts you or adding a splash of color to remind you of God's promises.

Trying new ways to encounter scripture can breathe life into faith when it feels stale. I remember talking with Rose, a friend from my church who felt spiritually dry for months. She was hesitant but agreed to try Divine Reading with our small group over the phone. Reading the same Psalm together, sharing what stood out, and sitting quietly before praying gave her a sense of connection she hadn't felt in years. One morning, she called me just to say, "I felt God's peace for the first time in ages." Sometimes all it takes is one new practice to wake up old joy.

Divine Reading isn't just for solo time; it can work beautifully in groups, whether at church, in your living room, or even over the phone with family or friends who live far away. If you lead a group, print or hand out bookmarks with the four steps listed, so everyone can follow along easily. Take turns reading the passage aloud, allow time for each person to share what stood out (if they want), then spend a few quiet moments resting in God's presence together before closing with prayer. There's no pressure to "perform"—just space for honest listening and sharing.

If you prefer practicing alone, keep written instructions nearby as a reminder of each step. Sometimes I carry a small card with the four words: Read, Reflect, Respond, Rest tucked into my Bible as a prompt. On days when I feel scattered or forgetful, having these cues at hand helps me slow down and listen rather than rush through.

Trying new approaches isn't about chasing novelty; it's about opening ourselves to fresh encounters with God right where we are. Whether you're coloring scriptures in your recliner, listening to dramatized readings over breakfast, or sitting quietly after reading a few verses, these practices invite God into your ordinary moments in ways that surprise and sustain you.

As this chapter draws to a close, remember there's no single right way to build your spiritual foundation. What matters most is finding habits that fit your life now—habits that help you notice God's presence in new and deeper ways. In the next chapter, we'll look at how to find lasting purpose beyond the routines of work and daily tasks, discovering how faith shapes every season ahead.

Chapter 3 Finding Purpose Beyond the Workplace

"And whatever you do, whether in word or deed, do it all in the name of the Lord Jesus, giving thanks to God the Father through him."
— *Colossians 3:17 (NIV)*

Serving as a Prayer Warrior—Interceding for Family and Community

For much of my life, my purpose seemed wrapped up in what I did—my job, my responsibilities, the roles others expected me to fill. But when the career ended and the calendar cleared, I found myself asking, *Now what?*

Colossians 3:17 reminds me that purpose doesn't retire. It simply shifts. Whether I'm mentoring a grandchild, volunteering at church, or offering a listening ear to a friend, every act—big or small—can become sacred when done in Jesus' name. My life still matters. My impact still counts. And my purpose? It's just beginning to unfold in a whole new way.

If you asked me twenty years ago what kind of difference I wanted to make in retirement, I might have pictured myself leading a committee or volunteering at the library, not sitting quietly in my favorite chair. But as the years passed, I realized that some of the most important work God calls us to doesn't require standing at a podium or walking the halls of a hospital. It's the unseen ministry of intercessory prayer—lifting up people, needs, and even whole communities to God, often without them ever knowing. This practice isn't just for a select few. It's an open invitation for all of us, especially now, when the pace slows down and we find more moments of stillness. In these golden years, you can wield a spiritual influence that outlasts any title or job.

Intercessory prayer is simply praying on behalf of others. The Bible gives us beautiful models—think of Anna, the elderly prophetess who spent decades in the temple, praying and watching for God's promises (Luke 2:36-38). Anna was not up front giving the sermons; her quiet prayers were her gift to Israel. Epaphras, mentioned in Colossians 4:12, is another example—Paul describes him as "always wrestling in prayer" for his friends. These faithful servants became spiritual anchors for their communities. Their prayers shaped destinies even when they themselves stayed behind the scenes.

I've met retirees who have prayed for a wayward child for years, only to see hearts softened, or who regularly intercede for their church's youth group and later hear stories of young people choosing faith over despair. These stories aren't rare—they're reminders that God still works powerfully through the prayers of His people.

For those new to this kind of ministry, or needing a little structure to keep going, I've found that organizing your prayer life makes a big difference. Creating a prayer list or journal helps you stay intentional. Some folks keep a simple notebook with names and specific requests. Others get creative—index cards for different days of the week, or color-coded lists for family, friends, leaders, and missionaries. When you check off answers or make notes about changes, it becomes a living testimony of God's faithfulness over time. If you enjoy connecting with others, setting up a weekly prayer call keeps you motivated and accountable. You might invite a friend or two—agree on a time to pray together by phone or even video chat. This doesn't have to be formal; just share requests and lift them up together. Many churches have directories or missionary newsletters that serve as rich guides for your prayers. Flipping through those pages, you can pray for each name, face, or ministry—even if you've never met them in person.

One beautiful part about intercessory prayer is how it lets you affect people and places far beyond your reach. Your prayers can cover grandchildren's schools, bless teachers you'll never meet, or surround local leaders facing tough decisions. I've heard of grandparents who keep photos of their grandkids' school buildings and pray over them before class starts each week. Some retirees dedicate time each month to pray through headlines or community needs: local fire stations, hospitals, churches in transition. The impact ripples outwards—one woman I know prayed faithfully for her neighborhood for years; later she discovered several neighbors had come to faith during that season without ever knowing she was interceding for them. Prayers become part of your spiritual legacy—something your children and grandchildren will inherit even if they don't witness it firsthand.

Of course, there are seasons when prayer feels dry or discouraging. Sometimes it seems like nothing changes no matter how many times you ask God to move. When this happens, using scripture as prayer prompts can reignite your hope. Choose verses like

Philippians 4:6-7 ("Do not be anxious about anything...") or Psalm 91 ("He who dwells in the shelter of the Most High..."), and pray those words over your loved ones. You can rotate your prayer focus—one week praying for family, another for your church community, another for global needs—to keep things fresh and avoid feeling stuck. When words run out, silent prayer is just as meaningful; God hears what you cannot say.

Interactive Element: Creating Your Personal Prayer Map

Take out a piece of paper and draw circles for the people and groups God places on your heart—family names in one cluster, friends in another, church leaders elsewhere. Add schools, local organizations, or world regions if you feel called. Each week, pick one cluster to focus on. As you pray, jot down any updates or answers right on the map. Watch as it fills with notes and reminders that God is at work through your faithful intercession.

Embracing this overlooked ministry gives your days deep meaning and echoes long after you've whispered amen. Even now, as you read this, know that every prayer matters more than you may ever see in this life.

Small Acts, Big Ministry—Phone Calls, Cards, and the Gift of Encouragement

Not every ministry needs a pulpit or a crowd. Sometimes the greatest impact comes from the comfort of your kitchen table, with a pen in hand or a phone pressed to your ear. I've discovered that a simple phone call or a handwritten card can mean the world to someone who feels forgotten. In times marked by isolation, these small gestures hold immense power. God calls us to "encourage one another and build each other up" (1 Thessalonians 5:11), and you'd be surprised how often a gentle word or a friendly note arrives as an answer to prayer.

I remember hearing about a widow at church who lost her husband during the pandemic. She lived alone, her world suddenly smaller, her days quiet. One of our members started calling her every Tuesday afternoon—just to check in, share a little news, and remind her she wasn't alone. Over time, those calls became a highlight of her week. She confessed, "Sometimes I feel invisible, but your voice pulls me back into the light." That's the miracle of encouragement: it doesn't just fill a lonely hour, it restores hope and dignity.

Getting started with encouragement ministry is easier than you might think. Take out your church directory or jot down the names of neighbors you haven't seen in a while. Pick a handful to call or write each week. If lists help you, keep a simple log with names and dates so no one gets overlooked. Some folks like to create an "encouragement calendar"—a pocket calendar or notebook with names assigned to each day or week. You can circle back each month, spreading kindness across the calendar and giving yourself a gentle nudge to keep going. For those who enjoy company, consider inviting friends to join you in this ministry. A card-writing group can meet over coffee, or even coordinate by mail, each member choosing several recipients and mailing out cards on a set schedule.

Intention makes all the difference. Before picking up the phone or starting a note, pause for a moment of prayer. Ask God for words that comfort and for wisdom to know what each person needs. Sometimes I include a favorite scripture—a line from Psalms or Isaiah—or share the chorus of an old hymn that brings me peace. Personal stories help too; telling how God carried me through a tough patch reminds others that they're not alone in their struggles. When writing a card, I often recall specific memories: "I remember your kindness at last year's potluck," or "Thinking of how your laughter filled the hall." That bit of personal connection can turn a simple message into something treasured.

There's something sacred about timing. More than once, I've mailed a card only to find out later it arrived on an especially hard day. One woman told me she'd been in tears when my note landed in her mailbox, and she read it over and over all week. Another friend admitted he kept my voicemail saved on his phone for months, replaying it when he felt discouraged. These aren't grand gestures; they're reminders that God sees us and uses ordinary people—us—to bring His love in tangible ways.

If you want to expand your reach, get creative. Consider including uplifting poems, printed prayers, or even small bookmarks with verses. Some people tuck in pressed flowers or photos from church gatherings to remind recipients of happier times. You don't need fancy supplies; sincerity is what matters most. For those who are more tech-savvy, sending short voice messages or emails can work just as well, especially for those who may be hard of hearing or prefer reading over talking on the phone.

Sometimes encouragement becomes a two-way street. I've had folks call me back after receiving a card, their voices lighter as they share their own stories or ask how they can pray for me in return. It's more than ministry—it's friendship deepening across miles and seasons. Even if you never hear back, trust that each act plants seeds you may never see grow.

Reflection Section: Your Encouragement Toolkit

Take five minutes now to jot down three names—people who might need encouragement this week. Write one way you could reach out: call, card, email, or even a doorstep visit if possible. Ask God to bless these small acts and open your eyes to new opportunities. Keep this list handy and update it as God brings new people to mind.

In these years when energy sometimes wanes and crowds seem farther away, encouragement ministry shines bright. Small acts take on big meaning when offered with love and prayerful intention. Your voice, your words, your willingness to reach out—they all matter more than you know.

Volunteering with Limited Energy—Matching Service to Your Strengths

"Each of you should use whatever gift you have received to serve others, as faithful stewards of God's grace in its various forms."
— *1 Peter 4:10 (NIV)*

There was a time when I could say yes to everything—early mornings, long shifts, back-to-back commitments. But these days, my body has its own rhythm, and energy comes in shorter supply. I used to feel guilty for doing less... until I remembered that God never asked me to do it all—He simply asked me to be faithful with what I have.

1 Peter 4:10 reminds me that service isn't about stamina; it's about stewardship. Maybe I can't run the event, but I can send encouraging notes. Maybe I can't volunteer every week, but I can pray faithfully for those who do. God honors every act done in love. When we serve from our strengths, even small offerings become powerful blessings.

I know firsthand how retirement can bring a new set of questions about what you can realistically give. Some days, energy is a precious commodity. The body reminds you, in ways both loud and subtle, of its boundaries. Maybe you used to run church picnics or lead VBS, and now climbing stairs or standing for long periods can leave you exhausted. It's normal for your physical abilities to shift over time. That doesn't mean your days of meaningful service are behind you. On the contrary, it's a chance to discover what I call "right-sized" volunteering—serving in ways that suit your present strengths, not someone else's expectations or your own memories of the past.

There's no shame in admitting you can't do what you once did. I've talked with friends who felt frustrated when they had to step back from big commitments. Yet, many found fulfillment in smaller, sustainable roles. One neighbor of mine, who used to be a deacon, now finds joy assembling care packages from her kitchen table for folks who are homebound. Another friend, who tires easily, volunteers as a virtual tutor for kids needing reading help—he logs into short video calls a few times each week, supporting young learners without leaving his recliner. These quieter forms of service don't make the headlines, but they absolutely make a difference.

Assessing your current strengths helps you focus on what's possible and life-giving. Start by asking yourself, "What energizes me now?" Maybe it's chatting on the phone, baking bread, or organizing files. Then ask, "What leaves me drained?" For some, large groups or noisy environments feel overwhelming, while others thrive on behind-the-scenes work. If you enjoy conversation but struggle with mobility, consider roles like phone check-ins for church members or helping with remote administrative work. If you're organized, offer to sort donations for a local ministry or help coordinate schedules for volunteers. For those who love to bake, making cookies or casseroles for community events or people in need can be a sweet way to bless others.

You don't have to hunt far for opportunities that fit your current capabilities. Many churches and nonprofits need volunteers to assemble care packages—think snacks, devotionals, and notes of encouragement for shut-ins or hospital patients. If you're comfortable with technology, virtual volunteering opens even more doors. Prayer hotlines and online tutoring programs welcome seniors ready to listen or share knowledge. Some churches need help updating their websites or newsletters; you can write articles or edit from home. Even baking breads or simple treats for ministry gatherings counts as service—every loaf and batch carries love.

The important thing is to celebrate what you can do and let go of regrets over what you can't. Sometimes I catch myself longing for the energy I had at forty-five, but then I remember: every season has its own offerings. Reframing your contribution as "seed planting" has helped me let go of the pressure to produce instant results. Maybe all you can do is deliver a homemade pie to a neighbor or spend ten minutes praying over a list of needs—that is enough. God multiplies the smallest acts in ways we may never see.

Presence matters more than productivity. I have seen the ministry of simply showing up—whether in person or virtually—make all the difference for someone lonely or discouraged. A short visit at a nursing home or a quick call with a shut-in delivers hope and dignity in ways grand gestures never could. Your willingness to listen, share a memory, or offer practical support carries the love of Christ into ordinary moments.

Self-Assessment Exercise: Finding Your Fit

Take a moment with pen and paper and jot down two lists: "What I enjoy doing right now" and "What feels difficult for me." For each strength, write one potential way it could bless someone else—baking could mean making treats for the food pantry; enjoying conversation could lead to regular calls with folks going through tough times; being organized might help with sorting donations or managing church records from your computer. Circle two items that excite you most, then reach out to your church office or a favorite charity and ask if there's a way to help that matches what you circled.

The key isn't pushing yourself to exhaustion but finding those right-sized roles that fit where you are today. The world doesn't always notice these quiet offerings, but heaven surely does. Every note written, every cookie baked, each prayer whispered is a seed sown in faith—and that is more than enough for this season.

Mentoring the Next Generation—Sharing Your Faith Story

"One generation commends your works to another; they tell of your mighty acts."
— *Psalm 145:4 (NIV)*

There's a light you carry that no young person can fake or rush, a gentle wisdom that's worn in like a favorite chair. The years you've lived, the storms you've weathered, the prayers you've whispered in the dark—these are treasures the next generation needs more than ever. Scripture paints this calling in bold strokes: "One generation shall commend your works to another, and shall declare your mighty acts" (Psalm 145:4). Paul urges older men and women to teach and encourage those coming behind them in Titus 2, not by preaching from a stage, but by letting life and faith speak through kindness, honesty, and presence. Seniors like you are irreplaceable as mentors, whether you have a dozen grandkids or none at all. Spiritual grandparents are needed just as much as biological ones. Your faith story is not just interesting background—it can become someone else's anchor.

Opportunities for mentoring are all around, though they rarely announce themselves. Maybe your church youth group is looking for someone willing to share how faith shaped difficult decisions or how God showed up in unexpected places. You don't need to have all the answers; sometimes just showing up and listening makes all the difference. If public speaking isn't your thing, you might "adopt" a younger family at church, praying for them quietly or sending notes of encouragement during stressful seasons. Even a quick chat after Sunday service or a brief check-in before a big exam can leave a lasting mark. Some seniors volunteer with women's groups or participate in "adopt-a-grandparent" programs in schools or community centers. Others find their place outside formal programs—offering a ride, sharing a meal, or inviting a young couple over for coffee and real conversation about life and faith.

Telling your story well takes some thought and humility. I've found it helps to sketch out a "testimony timeline."

Start by jotting down key moments—joys, losses, doubts, answers to prayer—along a simple line marking years or decades. This visual map helps you see patterns of God's faithfulness and spot connections with struggles younger folks may face today. When you do share, it's best to focus on experiences that meet people where they are now—like how God met you during unemployment, illness, or times when hope seemed thin. Younger generations aren't looking for perfect heroes; they want real stories of wrestling with faith and finding light in hard places. Sometimes it's more powerful to share times when you doubted or failed and how God brought you through.

Technology opens up new doors for sharing your legacy. If you're comfortable with a smartphone or tablet, consider recording short video messages or audio clips—maybe a story about an answered prayer, a favorite verse that carried you through, or even a simple blessing for your family. These clips can be shared privately or posted on church pages. Writing legacy letters is another powerful tool; pour out your heart on paper and pass it along to your children, grandchildren, or even church members you mentor. These letters don't need flowery words—just honest reflections on what matters most and what you hope they'll remember long after you're gone.

Stories from other retirees prove that this kind of mentoring matters. I once met a man named Harold who saw a young couple struggling in their marriage at church. He and his wife invited them over for dinner once a month—no lectures, just good food and gentle questions. Over time, the couple opened up about their fears and hurts.

Harold shared how he and his wife survived hard seasons by clinging to prayer and forgiveness, not magic solutions but daily choices. Years later, that young couple credited those evenings with saving both their marriage and their faith. I've heard from others who grew up listening to their grandmother pray aloud every night—a memory that stuck with them long after her voice was gone. One woman told me her grandfather's handwritten notes of encouragement got her through college when she wanted to give up; she kept those letters taped inside her closet as daily reminders of God's care.

If you feel unqualified or worry your story isn't dramatic enough, remember that faithfulness is what stands out most. It's not about fancy words but simply offering yourself—your mistakes as much as your victories—as evidence that God works in ordinary lives. You carry decades of experience that textbooks can't teach and podcasts can't replicate. More than anything else, your presence tells the next generation: "You're not alone—God's been faithful to me, and He'll be faithful to you too."

Leading or Joining a Senior Bible Study—Building Community

There's something special about studying the Bible with people who understand firsthand what it means to have silver hair, a creaky knee, or a heart that aches for grandkids. In this stage of life, you find that faith questions shift. You might read the same passage you heard as a child, but now it lands deeper—maybe with a note of longing, or a little more wisdom tucked in. Joining or starting a Bible study that's geared toward seniors is not just about learning scripture; it's about sharing life, laughter, and those quiet worries that only come with age. The fellowship that grows in these circles is unique—you sit side by side with folks who know what it means to lose friends, wrestle with health, and pray long prayers for their families. The bonds formed here often last for years, sometimes decades, and carry you through both celebrations and hospital stays.

If you've never joined a group like this before, you aren't alone. Many people feel nervous at first, especially if they're not used to speaking up or feel unsure about their Bible knowledge. The good news is, most senior studies are warm and welcoming. You can always start by quietly listening, then share a thought or two when you feel ready. If your church doesn't already offer a group for older adults, you could begin by putting out feelers. Mention your interest to pastors, jot a note in the church bulletin, or bring it up at a potluck. You'd be surprised how many others are waiting for someone else to say something first. If getting to church isn't easy or health concerns keep you home, technology makes it possible to join in from anywhere. I've seen groups thrive over conference calls or Zoom meetings—everyone gathers with a mug of coffee, scripture in hand, and the distance melts away.

Choosing the right study material matters. For seniors, it helps to pick topics that speak honestly to the realities of aging—questions about legacy, hope after loss, handling regret, or finding new purpose when routines change. Studies that focus on biblical characters who found fresh callings in their later years seem to resonate deeply. There are books and guides written specifically for senior groups, with large-print text and discussion prompts that don't assume everyone remembers Sunday school perfectly. Audio resources work well too; some groups listen together and pause the recording for discussion.

Flexibility is key when it comes to how these groups gather. Some rotate facilitators so no one feels all the pressure. Meeting outdoors under a shady tree or on someone's porch changes the atmosphere completely—conversation flows easier, and nature adds its own kind of peace. Others gather in living rooms or senior centers where everyone knows how to find the bathroom and the snacks. If vision is an issue, try reading aloud as a group or playing audio Bibles so everyone can follow along without straining their eyes. Some members use magnifying sheets or tablets to enlarge text; others bring favorite translations to compare how a verse sounds in different words.

The ripple effect from these studies goes beyond the meetings themselves. A friend told me her closest friendship started because she sat next to someone new at Bible study—years later, they still call each other every few days just to check in or share prayer requests. Another gentleman said his faith came alive again after decades of "coasting" because one question in the group challenged him to rethink how he trusted God with his worries about aging. These groups often become lifelines when someone faces surgery or loss; casseroles show up at the door unasked, and prayers are lifted up without fanfare. I've seen people who never thought of themselves as leaders step up to guide discussions, discovering gifts they didn't know they had.

There's also tremendous value in learning across generations when younger folks visit or join the group for a session here and there. Seniors bring steady faith and hard-won wisdom; younger members offer fresh questions and perspectives that keep everyone thinking. This blend creates solidarity—a sense that faith really is for every season of life, not just the young or the old.

If you're feeling hesitant about joining or starting such a group, know this: you don't need to be a Bible scholar or have answers for every question. Just bring your curiosity, your stories, your willingness to listen and share. That's all it takes to build something beautiful—one conversation at a time—where faith grows strong roots and friendship flourishes right alongside it.

Embracing "Encouragement Ministry"—Blessing Others from Home

"Therefore encourage one another and build each other up, just as in fact you are doing."
— *1 Thessalonians 5:11 (NIV)*

I used to think ministry had to happen at a church, on a stage, or in a mission field. But these days, I've discovered something sacred right here at home: the quiet, powerful ministry of encouragement. Whether it's a phone call to a friend, a handwritten note to someone grieving, or a whispered prayer for a neighbor—I've learned that lifting others up doesn't require travel or titles. It just requires a willing heart. 1 Thessalonians 5:11 reminds me that encouragement is holy work. And sometimes, a few kind words spoken from the kitchen table can echo farther than we'll ever know.

Encouragement ministry is a calling that often gets overlooked, but it can bloom beautifully in the later years of life. I see it as a way to bring light into the corners of other people's days without ever needing to leave home. Think of Barnabas in the book of Acts—the early church called him the "son of encouragement." His words and actions lifted up weary hearts, giving hope when others felt lost or discouraged. That same spirit is needed now, maybe more than ever. Retirement doesn't mean your influence is spent; in fact, you may find your ability to encourage grows as life slows down and you notice people's needs more closely.

You don't have to fit a mold to bless others from home. Some people love hands-on projects, while others feel most comfortable with words or quiet gestures. I know folks who put together "blessing bags" for neighbors or for local shelters—little care packages with snacks, socks, a note of hope, maybe even a small devotional. Others use their phones to record short prayer messages or scripture readings, sending them out to friends who need a boost. I've seen joy sparked by surprise care packages mailed to missionaries or shut-ins—a box filled with treats, puzzles, a homemade bookmark, and a simple reminder that someone cares. For those who miss gathering in person, organizing "virtual encouragement parties" by phone or video can be a lifeline. Invite a few friends to share good news, pray together, or simply laugh over old stories. Even brief moments of connection can ease loneliness and remind us we're part of a larger family.

Your unique gifts can shape this ministry in ways only you can offer. If you have a knack for words, handwritten notes containing original prayers or short poems can become treasures for those who receive them. Creativity has no age limit—sharing handmade crafts, baked goods, or memory albums can turn an ordinary day into something truly special. Some retirees with a gift for hospitality have started a tradition of baking extra loaves of bread or batches of cookies just to give away. Others put together photo collages or scrapbooks for friends facing difficult times, blending memories with encouragement. The key is to use what comes naturally. If you love music, recording yourself singing an old hymn and sending it by email could lift someone's spirits long after the song ends.

What's remarkable is how encouragement flows both ways. Giving blesses the giver as much as the receiver. I remember a season when I felt adrift—my calendar was empty, and aches and worries seemed to multiply. Then I started sending weekly notes to a few friends who were struggling. At first, it felt like such a small thing—just words on paper. But over time, I noticed my outlook shifting. Instead of dwelling on what I'd lost, I found myself searching for ways to lift others up. One friend wrote back to say my prayer had arrived on a day she almost gave up hope. Another told me my note was tucked inside her Bible and reread whenever anxiety crept in. Their gratitude ignited something in me—a sense of purpose that filled the gaps left by retirement.

Encouragement ministry doesn't require grand gestures or perfect timing. In fact, some of the most meaningful moments are born out of simple faithfulness—a listening ear, an honest compliment, a reminder that God sees and loves each person right where they are. Over time, these acts weave a tapestry of kindness that strengthens both you and those around you. It's never too late to start. Whether you're outgoing or quiet, creative or practical, your willingness to encourage can change lives—including your own.

As this chapter draws to a close, remember that purpose after retirement isn't found in busyness but in blessing others with what you have and who you are. Encouragement ministry is just one way God brings meaning into these years—through every note sent, every call made, every small act of kindness. Now, as we look ahead, we'll explore how faith can steady us through health changes and help us keep hope alive even when life takes unexpected turns.

Chapter 4 Navigating Loneliness and Grief With Christ

Naming Loneliness—Bringing Your Heartache to Jesus

"The Lord is close to the brokenhearted and saves those who are crushed in spirit."
— *Psalm 34:18 (NIV)*

Grief can come in quiet waves—sometimes expected, sometimes sudden. And loneliness, especially in this season of life, can settle in when the phone doesn't ring or the house feels too quiet. In those moments, I've often cried out, *"Lord, are You here?"* Psalm 34:18 reminds me that He is. Not watching from a distance, but close—intimately near the brokenhearted. I may not always feel Him, but I trust that He sits with me in the silence, collects every tear, and understands the ache no one else sees. With Christ, grief doesn't have the final word. His nearness becomes my strength, and His presence fills the emptiest spaces with peace I can't explain.

Loneliness often emerges during quiet afternoons, when the silence of a home stirs memories rather than conversation. Many of us have felt loneliness descend like an unwelcome heaviness—often more pronounced after life shifts with retirement or changes in relationships. It's easy to dismiss these feelings or shame ourselves for not being "grateful enough," but loneliness is real pain, not just fleeting sadness. If you're experiencing this, know you are far from alone. Nearly everyone encounters loneliness at some point in this stage of life.

Scripture does not ignore these emotions. The Bible is full of people who openly named their heartache. David gave voice to his sense of isolation: "Turn to me and be gracious to me, for I am lonely and afflicted" (Psalm 25:16). Elijah, exhausted and alone, called out to God in his despair. Honest prayers like these were not signs of weak faith—they were acts of trust, laying bare deep need before a God who listens. Lamenting is not outdated sadness; it's a spiritual practice that affirms and gives meaning to suffering. Naming your loneliness is not weakness or self-pity, but courage and the essential first step toward healing.

How can you express this pain in a way that leads to relief? Begin by allowing yourself to be honest with Jesus about what hurts. Writing a private letter to Him—honest, unfiltered, just as you feel—can be surprisingly freeing. For example, write what it feels like when dinner is quiet, or friends no longer call, or when you wonder if anyone would notice your absence at church. Putting these words on paper, even if Jesus already knows, often makes the weight lighter. If you haven't tried before, simply start: "Dear Jesus, today I feel…" and write as plainly as you can.

Another helpful practice is keeping a "feelings journal." This is not to dwell on sadness, but to notice patterns: when is loneliness most acute? After certain phone calls, during rainy evenings, or seeing photos of friends? Tracking these moments can reveal triggers and help you see how God meets you even there.

Sometimes, simply becoming aware is significant progress.

When loneliness feels overwhelming—late at night or when seeing people joyfully together—breath prayers can help soothe you. These are short phrases prayed in rhythm with your breath. For instance, breathe in: "Jesus." Breathe out: "Stay with me." Repeat until the anxiety settles. Simple, repeated prayers like these create spaces in which God's comfort can reach you even when words fail.

God's promise of presence is constant, even when we feel forgotten. Isaiah 41:10 reassures: "So do not fear, for I am with you; do not be dismayed, for I am your God." Jesus reaffirms it: "And surely I am with you always, to the very end of the age" (Matthew 28:20). These aren't just words—they're anchors for the loneliness that can be hardest to bear.

A woman from church once described her first weeks in assisted living. She felt invisible as people passed her room, everyone preoccupied. At her lowest moment, she prayed by her window in tears. Slowly, she felt a warmth—not physical, but within—a quiet assurance she wasn't alone. She started reading Scripture aloud at her window; over time, others lingered and joined her. By naming loneliness, she made space for connection and healing.

Interactive Element: Reflection Exercise—Bringing Loneliness to Jesus

Give yourself ten minutes to write Jesus a letter about how loneliness feels today. Be as honest as you can.

Afterward, read Isaiah 41:10 or Matthew 28:20 out loud. Close your eyes and repeat the breath prayer, "Jesus, stay with me," several times. Keep the letter somewhere special—maybe in your Bible—as a reminder that your pain matters to God.

Loneliness is not the end of your story—it's a place where God meets you with compassion and hope. The Psalms remind us that there's no shame in bringing our strongest feelings—even the hard ones—to Jesus.

Reaching Out When It's Hard—Practical Steps for Building New Friendships

Building new friendships in retirement can feel daunting—like standing uncertainly on the outskirts, unsure if anyone will notice or care. The biggest hurdle for many isn't wanting friends;

it's moving past the awkwardness, fear of rejection, or simply not knowing how to start. You might remember how naturally connections formed at the office, kids' activities, or social gatherings, but now, those routines have faded, and familiar faces are gone. Picking up the phone or walking into a new group can be intimidating. If you've ever felt that hesitation or heard the inner worry, "What if they don't want me?"—you're not alone.

Vulnerability is real, but so is the desire for connection. One way to move forward is by setting small, attainable goals. Instead of pressuring yourself to find a best friend quickly, start with brief, simple invitations—ask a neighbor for coffee, invite someone for a walk, or chat at the mailbox. Sometimes, sign up for one-time events, like a church activity or a local club, just to meet new people. Showing up is half the battle;

even if conversation is awkward at first, your presence signals openness. Consider joining a new group—a Bible study, book club, or hobby circle. One friend joined a "knitting and conversation" group, even though she didn't knit. She found that simply showing up led her to both learn a craft and make friends.

Volunteering is another helpful route. Whether you're serving at a food pantry, helping with church events, or delivering meals, shared tasks make introductions smoother and reduce pressure for small talk. If bigger commitments feel too much, offer to help with small event tasks like setup or clean-up—these are often where quiet friendships grow.

It's easy to talk yourself out of trying—worrying you'll have nothing in common, or say the wrong thing—but remember, most people in these groups are hoping for connection too. Many feel just as nervous as you. Don't let concerns about age or being different get in the way; genuine friendship goes beyond such boundaries.

If conversation doesn't flow naturally, come with a few open-ended questions. Try, "How did you get involved with this group?" or "What brought you here?" Simple compliments or sharing a story from your week can break the ice. When I joined an online faith forum (thanks to my granddaughter), people opened up quickly once someone reached out. Even digital spaces can nurture real friendships—one woman I met online became my pen-pal and prayer partner after only a few friendly messages.

Building new friendships takes patience and courage, especially if initial attempts don't succeed. Sometimes invites are declined or ignored—not because of you, but because others have their own fears or burdens. Don't let one setback stop you. Each try is practice in hope and openness.

For example, Martha, a retiree, hesitated for weeks before finally attending her local library's book club, promising herself just a cup of tea and cookies. That one step led to lasting friendships. Another gentleman found community online, exchanging phone calls and holiday cards with people he met in discussion forums.

If you're unsure where to begin, try these ideas:

- Attend a new group event at your church or community center.
- Enroll in a short-term class—art, gardening, writing.

- Volunteer even for just one event.
- Invite someone over for casual coffee or tea.
- Explore faith-based online forums or senior groups.

Connections often arise in small, unexpected ways—a shared joke, a compliment, or encouragement after a service. Every effort counts, even if you're nervous. What matters most isn't perfect conversation but simply showing up with a willing heart.

Facing Holidays and Anniversaries After Loss

Holidays and anniversaries, once bright with laughter and tradition, can turn bittersweet after a loved one is gone. These special days often stir up a storm of memories—sights, scents, even the way the light falls on an empty chair at the table. For me, that emptiness sometimes felt louder than any conversation, a silent echo that lingered all through the meal. Birthdays and milestones bring their own ache, marking both what was and what will never be again in quite the same way. You might find yourself anticipating these dates with dread, bracing for a wave of sorrow that rises when family gathers and the one you miss is not there to share it.

It's normal for tears to surface more easily during these seasons. Smiles can feel forced, while everyone else seems swept up in celebration. The pain may tighten around your chest when you set out the old decorations or hear that familiar song. Old photos and family recipes have a way of reopening wounds you thought had begun to heal. Even joy can feel tinged with guilt, as if you're betraying the memory of your loved one by laughing or enjoying yourself. The ache of longing only deepens when others assume you should have "moved on," or when well-meaning friends avoid mentioning your loss altogether.

There are gentle ways to let yourself grieve while still finding meaning in these days. One practice that brings comfort to many is lighting a candle in remembrance before a meal or gathering. As the flame flickers, say your loved one's name aloud or in your heart, inviting God's peace into the room. Setting aside a few moments for prayer or reading scripture together can also anchor the day in hope. Favorite passages—perhaps Psalm 23 or John 14—can be read aloud by yourself or with family, reminding you of God's presence even in sorrow.

Adapting old traditions or creating new ones can help transform painful anniversaries into opportunities for gentle healing. It might be as simple as preparing your loved one's favorite dish and sharing a story about them as you eat. Some find it meaningful to volunteer on these hard days—serving at a soup kitchen or delivering meals—turning grief outward into compassion for others. A quiet act of kindness can shift your focus from emptiness to purpose, even if just for an afternoon. If words fail you in person, writing a letter to your loved one offers another outlet. Pour out your current feelings—tell them what life looks like now, what you miss most, how their memory shapes your days. You might tuck the letter into a Bible or place it somewhere special.

Seeking support is vital when holidays feel overwhelming. Isolating yourself may seem easier, but reaching out can change everything. Attending a church service of remembrance—even if you slip in quietly at the back—reminds you that yours is not the only heart missing someone today. Many churches and communities hold special gatherings for those who grieve during the holidays, where candles are lit and names spoken aloud in prayerful solidarity. If gathering in person feels too hard, consider connecting with a grief support group—whether through your church, a local center, or even online. Listening to others share their stories helps break the silence of sorrow and brings unexpected comfort.

Reflection Section: Gentle Adaptations for Difficult Days

Try listing three simple ways you might honor your loved one's memory next holiday or anniversary. Maybe it's preparing their favorite dessert, volunteering an hour at a local charity, or setting a place at the table with flowers and a photo. Write down one scripture or prayer that brings you peace—keep it nearby for those moments when emotions surge.

Grief will change how these days feel, sometimes from year to year. Give yourself grace to adapt traditions as needed. Some years you may want to gather with family; other years, solitude might feel right. Let go of expectations—your way of honoring and remembering doesn't have to match anyone else's. Over time, small rituals can soften pain and offer new meaning, helping you hold both loss and hope side by side as you mark these sacred days.

Grieving with God—Honest Lament and Biblical Hope

"My soul is downcast within me; therefore I will remember you."
— *Psalm 42:6a (NIV)*

There are days when my soul feels heavy—when memories stir tears, and loss feels louder than joy. In those moments, I've learned not to hide my sorrow from God, but to bring it to Him raw and unfiltered. Psalm 42 gives me permission to grieve with honesty. It reminds me that faith isn't pretending everything is okay—it's remembering God even when it's not. "My soul is downcast... therefore I will remember You." Grief and hope can coexist. God doesn't ask us to skip the pain; He simply invites us to walk through it with Him. And in that sacred space, where lament meets trust, healing begins.

Grief can feel intensely physical—like heaviness in the chest or persistent exhaustion. Many believe faith means masking pain, but the Bible tells a different story. Scripture is filled with people who brought their sorrows openly before God, trusting He could handle their tears. Lament is not weakness but sacred honesty. King David's psalms are full of raw anguish: "Why are you downcast, O my soul? Why so disturbed within me?" (Psalm 42:5). These words are unvarnished and real. Even Jesus grieved openly in Gethsemane, pleading with the Father, and weeping as He prayed. If Jesus Himself could express grief, so can we.

Grief often leaves us wordless—sometimes all we have are sighs or groans. Other times, it shows up as hard questions: "Why did this happen?" "Where were You, God?" Lament isn't pretending everything is okay; it's speaking the truth of our hurt while trusting God won't turn us away. Your prayers don't have to be polished—just genuine. Take time to write your own psalm of lament: begin by naming what hurts most, in plain words. Ask your questions, express complaints if you need to, and, like David, end with a line of hope, even if it's tentative: "But I know You hear me." "I trust You're near, even now." Giving voice to grief in this way helps open the door to healing.

When prayers run dry or feel difficult, praying through the psalms can help. For hard days, Psalm 13 is a fitting companion: "How long, Lord? Will you forget me forever? ... But I trust in your unfailing love." Psalm 42 also gives language to deep sorrow: "Deep calls to deep ... all Your waves and breakers have swept over me." Read these psalms aloud; let their ancient honesty shape your own prayers. If you don't know where to start, pick a verse that speaks to you and use it as a prompt: "Today my soul thirsts for You because…" Let the psalms give you words until you find your own.

Grief can feel like wandering in a fog with no escape. The world may expect us to "move on" after a while, but true healing isn't linear. Some days you might feel capable, while other days bring unexpected tears—a song, a photo, an empty chair. Give yourself permission to grieve at your own pace, with no apologies and no set timeline. Some losses leave scars that ache long after others believe you should be "over it."

Faith does not make grief disappear, but it offers hope even in sorrow. Paul reminds us, "We do not grieve as those who have no hope" (1 Thessalonians 4:13). Hope is not denial; it's holding sorrow and promise together. Revelation 21:4 assures us God will wipe away every tear, and death will not have the final say. Sometimes hope feels distant, but even a faint glimmer is something to lean on when grief resurfaces. A friend who lost her brother held to that promise—not because hope was always strong, but because she needed something solid when sadness hit.

Hope can be found in small moments—a sunrise after a cloudy night, a warm hug, laughter over coffee. These glimpses don't erase pain but remind us that joy can return, even in brief flashes. If you are mourning, whether the pain is fresh or long-standing, remember it's okay to grieve for as long as you need. God meets us in our sorrow, not with lectures but with comfort and presence.

If you want a simple way to process your grief today, try writing your own lament using this outline:

1. Address God honestly
2. Name your sorrow and questions
3. Ask for help or comfort
4. End with hope or a trust in His presence, however small

Returning to scriptures about hope, like Revelation 21:4 ("He will wipe every tear from their eyes..."), can steady you when sadness returns. Give yourself room for both sorrow and hope; both are part of faith.

The Ministry of Presence—Finding Healing in Fellowship

There's a kind of healing that doesn't come from clever words or perfect advice. Sometimes, what soothes the soul most is simply being with someone—no speeches, no pressure to fix anything, just the comfort of company. In the Bible, this is made beautifully clear. When Job's life unraveled, his friends first sat beside him in silence for seven days and nights. They didn't try to explain away his pain or offer solutions; they just stayed close. Later, their words actually did more harm than good, but those early hours of quiet presence spoke volumes. Jesus also modeled this when He visited Mary and Martha after Lazarus died. He didn't arrive with a sermon but wept with them, sharing their sorrow before speaking hope.

When sorrow presses in, the presence of another person can be a lifeline. You don't need to fill the silence with conversation. Just letting someone sit with you on the porch, watching the wind move through the trees, or sharing a mug of tea at the kitchen table can say more than any words ever could. Sometimes, accepting a friend's offer to sit quietly together takes courage. It means letting down your guard and allowing someone else to witness your pain. Yet, this simple act can ease the ache just enough so you can breathe again. If you're the one reaching out, remember you don't have to plan an elaborate visit. A quiet afternoon watching old movies, working on a jigsaw puzzle together, or listening to music can bring comfort that goes deeper than conversation.

When talking feels impossible, shared activities or just being present in a group can create space for gentle healing. Church potlucks or small group gatherings aren't just about food or study; they're chances to be surrounded by warmth and familiarity. You might not feel ready to talk about your loss or even to smile much, but sitting in a room with others reminds you that you are part of something bigger than your grief. Even participating in a "silent walk" with a friend—a stroll through a garden or park without the need for chatter—can settle your spirit and remind you that you are not alone in the world.

I remember a man named Leon who lost his wife after sixty years of marriage. He found Sunday mornings unbearable at first, unable to face church alone. One week, a neighbor invited him to join her for coffee after service—not to talk about grief, just to sit together and watch folks come and go. Over time, Leon noticed that these quiet gatherings eased the sharpest edges of his sadness. He started looking forward to them, even on dark days. Another woman I know, Ruth, dreaded afternoons until a group from her congregation began visiting her every Thursday with crossword puzzles and cookies. They didn't pressure her to share her feelings; they just kept showing up. Their regular visits became anchors—steady reminders that she still mattered.

The gift of presence isn't something only others can give you; it's also something you can offer even when you feel empty yourself. You don't have to be cheerful or wise—just willing to show up and stay awhile. Inviting someone over for tea or offering to run errands together can be a way of saying, "You're worth my time." Sometimes, the smallest gestures—dropping off a casserole, sitting together in church, planting flowers side by side—open doors for healing.

Even when you find yourself unable to speak much at all, choosing to be present at community events matters. Maybe you attend a quilting circle or join others in the church kitchen for an afternoon of baking bread. You may not talk about your grief directly, but your heart senses the support around you. Shared hobbies create rhythms that anchor you—a knitting needle passed back and forth, or paintbrushes dipped in quiet concentration.

There's something sacred about knowing people will show up for you—not because they have answers but because they care enough to share the silence. That silent support becomes a thread connecting you back to life bit by bit. If you're struggling with loss right now, try saying yes to a simple invitation or extend one yourself. Even if it feels awkward at first, the comfort that comes with another's presence may surprise you.

A friend once told me about a weekly coffee group at her church where talking wasn't required—just being together was enough. Over time, she found herself laughing again and feeling lighter as new friendships formed naturally in those quiet hours. Another retiree shared how church friends took turns stopping by each week after his wife passed away—not for deep conversations but to share an afternoon walk or watch baseball on TV. Each visit stitched small patches of hope into his days.

Healing rarely happens all at once, and words are often overrated in times of deep pain. The ministry of presence—just showing up with open hands and a willing heart—has power to mend what words cannot reach.

Remembering Your Loved Ones—Creating Spiritual Legacies After Loss

The ache of missing someone you love doesn't fade just because time moves forward. Many days, you feel the urge to hold onto memories, not out of longing for the past, but to honor the person who shaped your life and faith. One way I found comfort was by creating a memory box. I gathered photos, handwritten notes, favorite recipes, trinkets, and Bible verses that spoke to our shared story. Tucking a little scripture beside a snapshot or a pressed flower from a special day turned a simple box into a sacred space—a place where I could sit quietly and remember. Sometimes I added a new note or verse when a special memory surfaced. Over time, this box became more than just storage. It became a reminder of God's faithfulness through my loved one's life.

Albums work just as well, especially if you enjoy arranging photos or jotting down stories in the margins. Include favorite scriptures next to pictures of family gatherings or baptisms, and make space for your own prayers or blessings. These albums don't have to be elaborate. It's the heart behind them that matters. You might even set aside one day each year as a personal day of remembrance—lighting a candle, reading passages like John 14:1-3 ("In my Father's house are many rooms..."), and spending time in quiet reflection or worship. This tradition can transform grief into hope, letting you mark the day with gratitude for what was and assurance of what's still to come.

Passing down stories and values keeps your loved one's influence alive for generations. Writing a "legacy letter" is one powerful way to do this. Take time to share what made your loved one special—their favorite hymn, their steadfastness in prayer, the way they showed kindness when no one was looking. You don't need fancy language; speak honestly about what you learned from them and how their faith shaped your family. A simple letter tucked in a Bible or mailed to grandchildren becomes a treasured gift, one they might return to in their own seasons of loss or doubt. If writing doesn't come easily, consider recording short audio stories on your phone or sharing memories over coffee with your family. My grandchildren loved hearing about their grandfather's quiet courage during hard times, especially when I described how he relied on prayer when answers were hard to find.

Inviting family and friends to participate in these legacy-building activities can bring unexpected healing and connection. Host a storytelling night—ask everyone to bring a memory or favorite photo and share what stands out most. These gatherings often bring laughter and tears, sometimes in the same breath. If your loved one cared about a particular cause or ministry, making a donation in their honor can turn loss into blessing for others. Even planting a tree or starting a small garden as a living memorial can bring comfort; each new blossom becomes a sign that love continues to grow, even in changed soil.

The hope of reunion is what sets Christian legacy apart from simple nostalgia. When Jesus promised, "I go to prepare a place for you..." (John 14:2), He offered assurance that those who trust Him are never truly lost to us. Death may separate us for now, but it isn't the end of the story. Sharing this hope with children and grandchildren, telling them about the faith that sustained both you and your loved one, plants seeds that can flourish long after we're gone. I've seen grandchildren deeply moved by stories of generosity or quiet faithfulness—those tales become part of their own spiritual heritage.

Over the years, I've heard testimonies from friends whose lives changed because someone took time to share memories and values rooted in faith. A neighbor once told me how she kept her grandmother's Bible by her bed, not just for the notes in the margins but for the sense of connection it brought. Another friend's granddaughter said learning about her grandfather's tradition of nightly prayer inspired her to start her own prayer journal—a legacy unfolding quietly but powerfully.

When we take time to remember our loved ones in these faith-filled ways, we do more than ease our own grief—we sow hope for those who follow us. Each story told, each letter written, each tree planted becomes a living testimony that love anchored in Christ endures beyond loss.

As this chapter draws to a close, remember that honoring those we miss isn't just about looking back—it's about carrying forward their faith and love into each new day. The legacies we shape in these quiet acts remind us that God continues working through our lives, even as we grieve. Next, we'll explore how faith can bring resilience and meaning when health challenges arise and physical strength is not what it once was.

Make a Difference with Your Review

Unlock the Power of Generosity

"True joy is not found in what we keep, but in what we give away in love—especially when no one is watching."
— Inspired by Matthew 6:3-4

People who give without expectation live longer, happier lives. So if we've got a shot at that during our time together, darn it, I'm gonna try.

Please help by leaving a review for this book.

Your gift costs nothing and takes less than 60 seconds to make a real difference, but it can change another person's life forever. If you feel good about helping others, then you are my kind of people. Welcome to the club. You're one of us. Thank you from the bottom of my heart. Now, back to our regularly scheduled programming.

- Your biggest fan, Ben A. Collingstone

PS - Fun fact: If you provide something of value to another person, it makes you more valuable to them. If you want to send goodwill directly to another reader and believe this book will help them, please share it with them.

Chapter 5 Faith Through Health Challenges

Trusting God with Your Body—Aging, Illness, and Divine Purpose

"Therefore we do not lose heart. Though outwardly we are wasting away, yet inwardly we are being renewed day by day."
— *2 Corinthians 4:16 (NIV)*

I never expected to become so acquainted with doctor's offices. For years, I took my body for granted—standing up easily, lifting groceries, tying shoes without effort. Then, suddenly, every movement required negotiation. Maybe you've bargained with aching joints or felt frustrated as your hands faltered. It's surprising how quickly your own body can feel unfamiliar. The same eyes meet you in the mirror, now framed by new lines and softened skin—reminders of a life well-lived.

It's natural to ask, "Why, Lord?" when illness or aging appear. I've whispered that question many times, especially during restless, painful nights. But this isn't weak faith—it's honest relationship with God. The Psalms are full of such questions. David and others brought confusion and sorrow to God. Psalm 139 reminds us God knows every cell, ache, and limitation: "You knit me together in my mother's womb... I am fearfully and wonderfully made." This truth doesn't fade as our bodies change. You are valued in every stage—strong or frail, energetic or weary. God delights in you even as your strength diminishes.

Aging doesn't mean God has forgotten you. Illness is not punishment; aging isn't failure. The Bible offers hope—Paul speaks in 2 Corinthians 12:9, "My grace is sufficient for you, for my power is made perfect in weakness." Paul lived with a persistent challenge—his "thorn in the flesh"—yet he didn't withdraw. Instead, he discovered God's grace most clearly when he reached his own limit.

Caleb, at eighty-five, sought new challenges from God and kept serving. Zechariah and Elizabeth, in their later years, received a miracle son and played a crucial role in God's plan. These stories are invitations, not exceptions—God still works through those who feel worn down or overlooked. Your present, imperfect body remains part of God's story.

The spiritual struggle isn't just pain or fatigue, but questioning what good can come from limitation. I've had to let go of certain dreams—like hiking specific trails or running with grandkids—but found unexpected gifts in slowing down. When I stopped fighting my body and asked God, "How can I serve from here?" new opportunities appeared. Prayers became deeper, conversations more honest, and simple garden walks became worship.

Surrendering to God is now part of my daily rhythm. Most mornings, I pray, "Lord, I accept what today holds and trust You to use it." Acceptance isn't resignation—it's making peace with reality and inviting God into each detail. If you're struggling to find purpose within limitation, consider what gifts you can offer today—listening, encouragement, prayer, or simply sharing your story with someone who also struggles.

Even as they change, our bodies remain temples of the Holy Spirit—wrinkles, scars, replaced joints and all. Honoring your body now may look different, but it's still spiritual. Gentle movement, like stretching while breathing deeply, or even moving your fingers, can be prayerful. Accompany stretches with whispered prayers—"Thank You for this breath," or "Strengthen me for what's ahead." If mobility is limited, even small motions while praying hold meaning.

Speaking truth over your body is vital. It's easy to slip into negative self-talk: "I'm useless," or "I look terrible." Instead, Scripture urges kindness—to others and to ourselves. Speak aloud: "I am beloved by God," "My body is a gift," or "God's strength holds me up." These aren't empty affirmations; they're biblical truths.

Reflection: Blessing Your Body

Take a moment today to write a short blessing for your body as it is now. Start with gratitude for what you can still do—a walk to the mailbox, holding a cup of tea, seeing the sunrise. Add a prayer for areas that ache: "Lord, thank You for my hands that still comfort others; please bring relief to these stiff knees." Read your blessing aloud each morning this week as an act of honoring God and yourself.

Caring for your body—no matter its condition—is reverence, not vanity. Every gentle movement and each kind word to yourself is an act of faith, recognizing God's presence in every breath and heartbeat.

Adapting Spiritual Practices for Limited Mobility or Memory

Losing the ability to do what once seemed effortless can bring heartache. I remember the first time I could no longer kneel beside my bed—the ache was more than physical. Maybe you've reached for a Bible and found the print too small, or struggled to recall a favorite psalm. Letting go of beloved habits like prayer circles, singing in the choir, or sitting through a full church service can sting, and it's normal to feel frustration or grief. You may even worry you're losing touch with God as routines slip away. I've felt that worry myself. But I've learned that faith isn't about doing more—it's about the persistence with which you keep showing up, even if "showing up" looks different now.

The first step in adapting spiritual practices is giving yourself permission to change. If long devotionals are exhausting, try a simple prayer: just a few lines said slowly, like "Lord, have mercy," or "Be near me today." Those who struggle with reading can turn to large-print devotionals or audio Bibles—hearing scripture read aloud can be even more meaningful than silent reading. If holding a book is tricky, prop it open or ask someone to record favorite passages in their voice. Visual aids help too—keep scripture cards with short verses around the house to catch your eye and heart throughout the day.

For moments when focus slips or memory fades, breath prayers offer comfort. Pair a brief phrase with breathing: inhale, "Jesus"; exhale, "be my strength." You don't need perfect words or memory—just the willingness to pause and rest in God's presence for a few breaths. Single-verse meditation is also a comfort: repeat a verse like, "The Lord is my Shepherd," letting each word settle in your heart. If memory is unreliable, even tracing the letters with your finger can help anchor the words inside you.

If cognitive changes are mild, adapt scripture memory techniques. Write a verse on an index card, keep it handy, and read it aloud morning and evening. Pair words with a gesture—touch your heart for "love," open your hands for "peace." Rhythm and repetition help cement the words. Many find that short scripture passages in song or chant linger longer than spoken words.

The heart of all this is maintaining your connection with God, not performing perfectly. It's tempting to feel guilty for "doing less," but faithfulness matters more than performance. A whispered prayer at noon can be as meaningful as the hour-long studies you used to do. One friend keeps a bell by her chair; each time she rings it, she offers a one-sentence prayer—no pressure, simply honest presence.

Don't hesitate to involve others in faith practices. Family members and caregivers can join you gently. Ask a grandchild to read scripture while you listen, or play hymns together as you go through daily tasks. Even sharing worship music can create sacred moments in ordinary afternoons. If you're alone, call a friend to pray together briefly over the phone.

Letting others in doesn't mean losing independence—it means finding new, shared ways to nurture faith. Children might enjoy reading a picture Bible or saying a simple prayer, and friends can share in brief devotions. These shared moments don't require stamina or perfect memory—just open hearts.

Adapting spiritual disciplines isn't giving up; it's about receiving grace for what's possible today. Faith meets you in whispered prayers, sung verses, and quiet listening—meeting you right where you are, without judgment.

Simple Routine Adaptation Checklist

- Choose one spiritual habit that feels heavy.
- Ask: "How could this be shorter or simpler?"
- Swap reading for listening, kneeling for sitting.
- Invite someone to share one practice with you this week.
- Notice what brings peace, and let go of what feels forced.

Faith doesn't diminish when habits change—it adapts and deepens, following you into each new season.

Asking for Help—Faithful Approaches to Accepting Support

"Carry each other's burdens, and in this way you will fulfill the law of Christ."
— *Galatians 6:2 (NIV)*

I'll admit, asking for help never came easily to me. Maybe you feel the same way. You've spent decades building your independence, raising children, holding down jobs, and caring for others. Suddenly, needing a hand with groceries or a ride to the doctor can stir up all kinds of emotions—pride, worry about being a burden, even embarrassment or shame. You might hear an old voice in your head saying, "Don't trouble anyone," or "Handle it yourself." I've heard those voices too.

I've spent much of my life being the one others could count on—strong, capable, dependable. But in this season, I'm learning that strength also means knowing when to reach out and receive.

Galatians 6:2 reminds me that we're not meant to carry everything alone. When I let someone else help—whether it's with a ride, a meal, or a listening ear—I'm not burdening them; I'm inviting them to live out the love of Christ. There is holiness in both giving and receiving. And when we allow others to walk beside us, we fulfill God's vision for a caring, connected body of believers. The truth is, these feelings are common. They're part of being human, especially in a culture that praises self-reliance. Yet, at some point, all of us need support—no one gets through life alone.

Even Jesus accepted help. Think about that for a moment. When He carried the cross and stumbled, Simon of Cyrene stepped in to carry it for Him. Jesus didn't refuse. He allowed others to serve Him in His moment of weakness. And when He visited Mary and Martha, He let them care for Him—He didn't insist on doing everything Himself. If the Son of God could accept support, maybe it's time we see help as a gift rather than a failure.

Scripture encourages us to carry one another's burdens (Galatians 6:2). That isn't just about helping others—it means letting others share our load too. When you allow someone to help, you give them a chance to serve and grow in love. It's not one-sided. The truth is, receiving help can bless the giver as much as the receiver. I remember when my neighbor insisted on mowing my lawn after my knee surgery. I wanted to protest, but something stopped me. Later, she told me it brought her joy to serve and gave us both a chance to become better friends. Your willingness to accept help opens doors for real community.

Still, asking can feel awkward. Sometimes you don't even know what words to use. I've found it helps to get specific and keep it simple: "Would you mind picking up milk and bread when you're at the store?" or "Could you drive me to my appointment next Thursday?" Even saying, "I'm having trouble with the trash bins—could you help me roll them out?" makes it easier for someone else to say yes. If you're reaching out to your church or a volunteer group, try: "I could use a little help with meals this week while I recover," or "Is there anyone available to pray with me over the phone?" People appreciate clarity.

Creating a "help request list" can take the pressure off when someone offers their support. Sit down and jot out a few specific things—groceries, prescription pick-up, rides to church, prayers for certain worries, or someone to sit with you during a long afternoon. That way, when someone asks, "Is there anything I can do?" you don't have to scramble for an answer. You can look at your list and share one or two practical needs.

Sometimes you might worry about imposing or want things done a certain way. It's okay to voice your preferences kindly: "Thank you for offering to cook—I can't eat much salt, but I'd love a simple soup," or "If you're able to visit in the afternoon instead of morning, that works best for me." Setting gentle boundaries shows respect for both sides.

Building your support network before a crisis helps more than waiting until things get overwhelming. I wish I'd done that sooner myself. Think about joining a church care team or signing up for a meal train if one is offered nearby. Some churches have groups that organize rides or phone calls for members who need extra support. It's also wise to keep a list of local resources handy—senior centers, transportation services, home health agencies, and community groups focused on older adults. Even if you never use all these options, knowing they exist brings reassurance.

No matter how prepared you are, reaching out takes courage. But I've learned people want to help—they just need an invitation. And the surprising thing? Every time you let someone in, you create space for deeper connection and mutual blessing. Needing help is not a weakness; it's an opportunity for grace to grow between people who care about each other.

Interactive Exercise: My Support Circle

Take a moment today to write down three people or organizations you could contact if you needed a hand this month. Next to each name, jot one specific way they might help—whether it's prayer, errands, company, or something else unique to your situation. Keep this list somewhere visible as a gentle reminder: asking isn't failing—it's inviting others into meaningful partnership and real community.

Praying Through Pain—Finding Jesus in Physical Suffering

"He was despised and rejected by mankind, a man of suffering, and

familiar with pain... Surely he took up our pain and bore our suffering."
— *Isaiah 53:3–4a (NIV)*

Pain has a way of shrinking the world down to the ache itself. Pain has a way of isolating us. When the body aches or illness lingers, it can feel like no one truly understands—not even those with the best intentions. But Isaiah reminds me that Jesus does. He is not distant from suffering—He is intimately acquainted with it.

When I pray through my pain, I'm not just talking to a healer—I'm talking to Someone who has felt what I feel. Jesus carried wounds of His own, not just on the cross, but throughout His life. He knows exhaustion, rejection, and physical torment. And because of that, my prayers don't fall into a void—they fall into the arms of a Savior who understands. In suffering, I've discovered a quiet closeness with Christ

I never knew before. My body may be weak, but my connection to Him has never been stronger.

When you're hurting, it can be hard to think about anything else. You might find it tough to settle your mind or even form a full prayer. I've been there—lying awake in the small hours, trying to string together words of comfort, only to give up and whisper, "Help, Lord." Sometimes that's all that comes out. And I'm convinced that's enough. The Bible assures us that when words fail, the Holy Spirit steps in. Romans 8:26 says the Spirit intercedes for us through wordless groans. Even your sighs and tears are prayers God understands.

When pain flares, long prayers can feel impossible. That's when breath prayers become a lifeline. These are short, simple phrases you repeat as you inhale and exhale. They anchor you when pain distracts and overwhelm sets in. Inhale, "Jesus, hold me." Exhale, "Carry me through." Or try a line from scripture—"The Lord is my Shepherd"—timed with your breathing. These tiny prayers can cut through the haze of discomfort and bring a surprising sense of peace. They don't require deep focus or lots of energy; they simply help you stay connected to God, one breath at a time.

Some days, even these short prayers might feel like a stretch. On those days, I turn to music. There's something about an old hymn playing softly in the background that calms the mind and soothes the spirit. The melody lingers, sometimes circling back hours later when pain returns. I know a woman who kept a playlist of favorite worship songs on her phone during her hospital stay; she told me the music reminded her she wasn't alone in those sterile rooms. Even listening quietly, without singing along, can draw your attention from pain to hope.

I once heard from a man named Tom who spent weeks in a hospital bed after surgery. The nights were long and restless, filled with strange sounds and endless beeping machines. He told me he started praying for others in the ward when sleep wouldn't come—his roommate, the nurses passing by, patients he'd never meet. In those dark hours, his own pain took on new meaning as he lifted up silent prayers for healing and comfort for strangers nearby. Tom said God met him there—not by taking away every ache, but by filling the room with a sense of purpose and invisible community.

When suffering stretches on and relief seems far away, it's natural to wonder if God still hears you. You might feel overlooked or abandoned in the struggle. But the story of Jesus is full of pain—He knows what it is to endure suffering in both body and spirit. Meditating on His experiences, especially His time in Gethsemane or on the cross, can bring unexpected comfort. He was not immune to agony or fear; He even cried out to God with words of anguish. Yet in His suffering, He drew close to those who hurt and made a way for healing deeper than anything medicine can provide.

There's something powerful about offering your pain as prayer for others. When pain spikes—maybe during a difficult procedure or at three in the morning—use it as a moment to pray for someone else facing their own battle. "Lord, use my struggle right now for someone who needs hope," you might say. It's a mysterious thing, but many have found that this act of intercession makes their own burden lighter. You're not just enduring; you're participating in a holy work that ripples beyond your room.

If you find it hard to connect with God in pain, consider keeping a small notebook at your side. Jot down names or needs as they come to mind; let your discomfort become fuel for compassion. Write out scripture verses that bring comfort—keep them by your bedside or taped to your bathroom mirror. Sometimes just reading them aloud is all you can manage, but it's enough.

Pain does not disqualify you from prayer or closeness with Jesus. If anything, it draws you into the heart of what faith truly means—trusting God when you don't have all the answers and letting Him meet you right where it hurts most. In these moments, every whispered plea and every sacred silence becomes part of an ongoing conversation with the One who knows suffering and promises never to leave you alone in it.

Hospital Rooms as Holy Ground—Witnessing in Medical Settings

I remember spending more days in a hospital than at home, feeling stuck in the midst of the hospital's unique rhythm—nurses moving at all hours, the steady beep of monitors, the hush of evenings. At first, I dreaded it. Life felt paused, confined between uncomfortable chairs and sterile walls. But as time passed, my perspective changed. Even in those clinical spaces, God's presence found ways to shine through. Hospitals and clinics can become quiet places of faith, much like the crowded streets where Jesus healed the sick or Paul brought hope from prison.

Ministry can fill the smallest hospital moments. Sometimes, just letting my worn Bible sit on the bedside table prompted, "What are you reading?" from a nurse, opening gentle conversations about hope or survival. Having a devotional or hymn book handy invited others to share their thoughts. When a roommate seemed anxious, I'd offer, "Would you like me to pray for you?"—sometimes they accepted, other times just nodded, visibly calmer. These were open invitations, not pressure.

Encouragement travels far amidst worry. Hospital staff—doctors, nurses, techs, aides, janitors—carry unseen burdens. A simple "thank you" can unexpectedly lift their spirits. I made it a habit to thank staff for everything, big or small: an extra blanket, an encouraging word, a cup of ice chips. Occasionally, I left a note or card at discharge: "You made these hard days easier—bless you." One nurse kept such notes in her pocket for rough shifts. These small, thoughtful acts are seeds of kindness that brighten tough moments.

There's power in showing your faith through actions more than words. Letting gratitude and peace show—even when you're hurting—can make people curious about your source of strength. Sometimes, softly singing a hymn or sharing a comforting verse started conversations that lingered. Once, an orderly stopped by as I sang "How Great Thou Art"; it reminded him of his grandmother's prayers. Faith doesn't need a sermon—just visibility.

Not every day is easy. Some days are heavy with pain or anxiety, and sometimes simply getting through is enough. Yet, even then, God can use your presence to encourage someone else—maybe just by offering a smile to the discouraged or to someone who's overheard hard news across the curtain. These small gestures create ripples that go unseen.

I also discovered the blessing of spiritual support in the hospital. Most hospitals have chaplains trained to listen, pray, and comfort, regardless of background. At first, I hesitated to call one, feeling it was too formal or like admitting defeat. But after a particularly hard night, a visit from a chaplain and a simple, heartfelt prayer eased my fears and changed my perspective on seeking spiritual help.

Some hospitals offer worship services on Sundays or holy days, either in small chapels or through in-room TV. Even if you're too weak to attend, listening in can make you feel part of something bigger than your own pain. Ask about these services or request scripture or devotional readings from the chaplain. Often, hearing scripture read aloud breaks through the gloom.

If you want to encourage staff but don't know what to say, keep it simple: "You're making a difference," "I appreciate you," or "God bless you today." Leaving a note at discharge lets them know their care mattered. For fellow patients, quietly offering to pray before a meal or sharing a comforting verse can be a lifeline during lonely times.

Medical settings are rarely comfortable, but they're full of people searching for hope. With gentle witness—a prayer, a thank you, a softly sung hymn—hospital rooms can become holy ground, places where God's love quietly works in and through you.

Finding Community When Homebound—Staying Connected to the Body of Christ

It's hard to describe the ache of missing church when health or mobility keeps you home. Sundays used to mean handshakes at the door, voices rising together in song, and the comfort of familiar faces in the pews. Now, maybe, you find yourself watching the sunlight move across the living room carpet while the world gathers elsewhere. I know how easy it is to feel invisible in those moments. Several friends have told me about feeling left behind—like the parade is marching on without them. One woman said she almost stopped answering the phone because it seemed no one from her church remembered she was there. Another man admitted he missed the simple touch of someone's hand on his shoulder during prayer time. These stories are more common than we realize, and they remind us that the pain of isolation is real, not just imagined.

Yet, even from home, you can remain woven into the life of God's people. Technology has opened doors we couldn't imagine before. Many churches now offer virtual Bible studies or prayer groups, and even if computers feel intimidating, a simple phone call can let you join a "phone church" where participants listen to worship services together. Some folks set up their TV or tablet to stream Sunday services. You can sing along with familiar hymns or simply rest in the prayers and readings, trusting that you're sharing sacred time with others—even if you can't see their faces.

If you need a more personal connection, try organizing a "porch visit" or a window wave with friends or family. You'd be surprised how much joy a five-minute chat from the porch or a wave through the window can bring. I've heard from people who arrange regular outdoor visits with friends—everyone sits a safe distance apart, but laughter and prayer still flow freely. Even short visits remind you that you're not forgotten and that your story still matters.

Staying connected is not just about what you receive but how you can reach out to others who may also feel unseen. Starting a homebound encouragement ministry is simpler than it sounds. Gather some cards or note paper and write short messages—scripture verses, memories, or simply "Thinking of you today." If writing isn't easy, record a short prayer or blessing on your phone and send it to someone else who can't get out much. These small acts build spiritual bridges. One friend keeps a list of fellow shut-ins and tries to reach out to one person each week. He says knowing he's brightening someone else's day gives him purpose and lifts his own spirits.

Don't be afraid to ask your church for support—often, folks want to help but don't know what's needed unless you speak up. Requesting communion delivery or a short home visit can make a world of difference. Many churches have volunteers who bring the Lord's Supper to those who can't attend in person; just call the church office and put your name on the list. If you'd like regular check-in calls, ask to be matched with someone from the congregation or a deacon willing to call once a week. These calls are more than just social—they're lifelines, helping you remain anchored in community.

If your church isn't already offering these supports, suggest starting them. Even a simple phone chain—where each person calls another every few days—creates a web of care that keeps everyone connected. You might also ask about receiving church bulletins by mail or email, so you can keep up with prayer needs and upcoming events.

Staying part of the Body of Christ while homebound takes effort from both sides, but it never has to be all on your shoulders. Sometimes your simple request opens the door for others to serve in ways they hadn't considered before. And when you reach out—to offer encouragement or ask for prayer—you remind yourself and others that every member is valuable no matter where they are.

Reflection Exercise: Community Connection Map

Draw a small map of your support network. Place yourself at the center, and add names of friends, family, church contacts, neighbors, and anyone else who brings comfort or support. Identify one person you haven't spoken to in a while—reach out this week with a note or call.

To sum up, being homebound changes how community looks but doesn't erase your place in it. Creative connections, honest communication, and small acts of reaching out keep you knit together with God's people. In the next chapter, we'll explore how faith shapes our legacy—how even from home, your influence can ripple through generations with love and wisdom.

Chapter 6 Overcoming Fear, Anxiety, and Spiritual Doubt

"What If?"—Faith Over Fear in Uncertain Times

"When I am afraid, I put my trust in you."
— *Psalm 56:3 (NIV)*

Fear doesn't always come with flashing lights or loud warnings. Sometimes it creeps in quietly—through a late-night worry, a sudden health scare, or an uncertain future. I used to think strong faith meant I shouldn't feel afraid. But over time, I've learned that fear is human—and faith is choosing to trust God anyway.

Psalm 56:3 reminds me that it's okay to feel the fear, as long as I don't stay there. Each time anxiety rises, I try to pause and whisper, "I trust You, Lord." Not because I have all the answers, but because I know the One who does.

Even in my doubts, He is patient. Even in my fears, He is faithful. Trust isn't always loud—it can be a quiet surrender, one breath at a time.

Affirmation:

"When I am afraid, I will trust in You. Your perfect love drives out fear. You are my refuge, my strength, and ever-present help in trouble. I will not be shaken."

(Inspired by Psalm 56:3, 1 John 4:18, Psalm 46:1, and Psalm 62:6)

The "what ifs" seem to gather as night falls. I expected them to quiet after I retired, but instead, they grew louder. Retirement brings not just a new schedule, but a host of new questions. What if my health fails? What if my spouse gets sick? What if I lose friends? What if my mind dulls? The questions multiply in the silence, each one easy to tug until it unravels sleep. Some mornings, I'd wake with tightness in my chest, mind racing about doctor reports, troubling family calls, or persistent aches I hoped would disappear. I know you've felt it too—the anxiety about the future and what you can't control.

These fears aren't unique; they're part of being human, especially as we age and life feels more fragile. The Bible doesn't shame us for feeling fear. In fact, "Do not fear" or "Fear not" appears more than three hundred times in Scripture. God knows our struggles and invites us to bring our worries into His light rather than letting them grow unchecked (Fear Not: 15 Bible Verses About Overcoming Fear, n.d.). I found that naming my fears, instead of hiding them, eased their hold on me.

A practical technique that helped was making two columns on a plain sheet of paper. On one side, I wrote every "what if" that troubled me—big or small. On the other, I matched each worry with a promise from Scripture. For health, Isaiah 41:10: "Do not fear, for I am with you." For family concerns, Psalm 138:8: "The Lord will fulfill His purpose for me." For loneliness, Hebrews 13:5: "I will never leave you nor forsake you." This didn't erase my fears, but it brought them into the open, where God's truth could meet them.

If you want to try this, set aside five minutes to do your own "fear inventory." Jot down your "what ifs" without filtering. Then look up promises—Psalms, Isaiah, or find some on cards from a bookstore. Match each worry with a verse. Put this list somewhere you'll see it—by your mirror or favorite chair. Read the verses out loud when anxiety creeps in.

Anxious thoughts can become mental ruts, like water carving stone. To redirect them, I posted short, reassuring verses where I'd see them—on the fridge, dashboard, even in my wallet. Psalm 56:3 is a favorite: "When I am afraid, I will trust in You." I used it as a breath prayer: inhale, "When I am afraid;" exhale, "I will trust in You." Try this simple prayer at the doctor's office, late at night, or while waiting for news.

Stories of others finding God's faithfulness can also help. My friend June had heart issues last year that filled her with dread as she awaited test results. She used breath prayers, quietly repeating, "Jesus, hold me close." She didn't get all the answers she wanted, but found a peace she couldn't explain. Later, she said she felt God's presence most in those anxious moments. Another friend was constantly worried about his grown children. Realizing anxiety didn't help, he started praying for them by name for ten minutes each morning, jotting their names and Bible promises on sticky notes near his coffee pot as a daily act of letting go.

Interactive Element: "What If" Faith Inventory

On a sheet of paper, create two columns labeled "My What Ifs" and "God's Promises." List every worry or fear you're carrying, no matter how small. For each, search for a comforting Bible verse or phrase. Post your inventory where you'll see it daily as a reminder that you're not facing these questions alone.

Fear will keep knocking, especially during uncertain times. But you don't have to let it take over. Each time you name your fears and pair them with God's promises, even if you do it quietly or shakily, you choose faith over fear. No matter how tentative your prayers, God meets you exactly where you are.

Trusting God with Financial and Security Concerns

"And my God will meet all your needs according to the riches of his glory in Christ Jesus."
— *Philippians 4:19 (NIV)*

For decades, I lived by spreadsheets and strategy, rising early and staying late to climb the ladder. I was a senior executive—respected, rewarded, and, by most standards, successful. I believed that if I just earned enough, saved enough, invested wisely enough, I could outrun worry. That money would insulate me from life's storms. But then came retirement. The title faded, the inbox went quiet, and I was left with... questions. Not just about finances, but about *security*. About who I was without the paycheck. And whether I had built my foundation on something eternal—or just on numbers.

Philippians 4:19 cut through the noise of my well-planned life: "And my God will meet all your needs..." Not *my career*, not *my portfolio*—but *my God*. Suddenly, I saw that true provision isn't found in controlling every outcome, but in trusting the One who holds all things, including me. Now, I still value stewardship. But I've surrendered the illusion that money is my safety net. God is. And in that, I've found peace that no pension ever promised.

I never expected the question "Will I have enough?" to echo so loudly in retirement. I planned, saved, and tried to be wise, but now, with each new bill or grocery run, a small knot forms in my stomach. When the mailbox brings another insurance notice or a medical statement, my mind can jump straight to worry. You might know that feeling—the unease about what's left in the checking account, or the fear that a single crisis could undo years of careful saving. Even if you've been prudent, it's easy to wonder: what if all those years of work aren't enough when a big expense hits? The reality is, as we age, costs for healthcare can spike, and the thought of becoming a burden on family can keep us up at night. Maybe you've whispered prayers in the dark: "Lord, will I run out? Will I have to move? Who will help if I need long-term care?"

Jesus knew people worried about these things. In Matthew 6:25–34, He spoke of sparrows and wildflowers—creatures that don't stockpile or stress, yet God feeds and clothes them. He asked, "Aren't you worth much more?" That question can feel almost too tender when bills are due or when you're watching every penny. Still, there's a comfort in remembering that our Heavenly Father sees each need before it even surfaces. This doesn't mean we ignore reality or stop planning; it means we hold our concerns up to God's promises and let Him carry some of the weight.

One practice that has helped me is creating what I call a "gratitude budget." Instead of only tracking what leaves my account, I note what comes in and what God has provided—pension deposits, Social Security, a neighbor's homemade soup, a grandchild's laughter on the porch. These gifts may not pay the mortgage, but they remind me that provision is more than just numbers on a statement. Each line becomes a small thank-you note to God for daily bread. Taking time to look at not just what's lacking but what's present can shift your heart from fear to gratitude. Try making your own list—write down every source of blessing or support you've received this month. You might be surprised by how many ways God is already showing up.

Another way to surrender financial anxiety is by inviting God into money matters directly. There are days when I sit at the kitchen table with my stack of bills and simply pray, "Lord, you see these numbers. You know my needs better than I do. Show me what to do." Sometimes I lay my hands right on the bank statement and ask for wisdom before making decisions about spending or giving. Before any purchase—big or small—I pause and say, "God, is this wise? Will this bring peace?" That simple habit has spared me from impulsive buys and helped stretch my resources further than I thought possible.

Prayer doesn't always change circumstances overnight, but it does bring a sense of partnership with God. You're not facing these decisions alone. Practical steps matter too—reviewing expenses, finding trustworthy advisors, asking your church about resources for seniors—but none of those efforts replace the peace that comes when you hand over your anxieties in prayer.

I've seen God's faithfulness in seasons of scarcity. There was a year when my neighbor's medical bills piled up higher than her income could cover. She swallowed her pride and shared her struggle at church. Within a week, an envelope from the benevolence fund arrived—enough to cover three months' medication and groceries. Tears streamed down her face as she realized she wasn't invisible and that God saw her need through others' generosity. Another friend, recently widowed and living on less than she ever imagined, found herself growing more generous instead of more fearful. She started giving small amounts to a food pantry each month, telling me that letting go of her grip on money gave her a deeper sense of contentment than any full bank account ever had.

Security isn't only about numbers; it's about trust—trust that God knows your needs and cares deeply for every detail. That trust grows with every prayer over a bill and every decision made with wisdom and hope instead of panic. Even when resources seem stretched thin or the future looks uncertain, God's provision often arrives in unexpected ways—a check from an old friend, a discount on a prescription, an invitation to share a meal.

If worry about finances is weighing you down tonight, take a moment to name those fears and lay them before God. Remember the sparrows and the lilies—not because their lives are easy, but because they're under God's constant watch. So are you. Your worth isn't measured by your balance sheet but by the love of a Father who promises to provide for today and every day ahead.

Battling the Fear of Dependency—Seeing Weakness as a Place for God's Strength

"But he said to me, 'My grace is sufficient for you, for my power is made perfect in weakness.' Therefore I will

boast all the more gladly about my weaknesses, so that Christ's power may rest on me."
— *2 Corinthians 12:9 (NIV)*

I used to pride myself on being the strong one—the one who didn't need help, who could lift the heavy boxes, solve the problems, and carry the weight for others. But aging has a way of peeling back that illusion. There are days now when I need a hand getting up, a reminder on the calendar, or someone else to drive me where I used to go freely.

At first, I fought it. Dependency felt like defeat. But then I encountered the words of Paul: "My power is made perfect in weakness." Suddenly, weakness didn't feel like failure—it felt like an invitation. An invitation to let go of the myth that I must always be self-sufficient... and to discover a deeper strength that is not my own.

God doesn't turn away from our limitations—He meets us there. And in the space where my strength ends, His grace begins to shine. Maybe being dependent isn't the end of dignity. Maybe it's the beginning of divine connection.

The thought of losing independence kept me awake more than once. Maybe you've felt it, too—a creeping worry that someday you might need help with simple things, or that asking for support will somehow shrink your dignity. It's easy to wonder, "Will I still have control over my life?" or, "What if I become a burden?" These questions rattle around, especially when the body starts saying no or when friends move to assisted living. Our society praises self-reliance, so needing help almost feels like a failure. I struggled with that for a long time. I hated asking for rides after I stopped driving, and I felt embarrassed when my hands shook too much to open jars at home. For decades, I was the one others relied on. Now, the roles started shifting, and I had to face the uncomfortable truth that my value couldn't be measured in how much I could do alone.

Scripture doesn't shy away from weakness; in fact, Paul writes in 2 Corinthians 12:10 that he "boasts in weakness," because it is there that Christ's power rests on him. That was a hard lesson for me. I wanted to be strong, but God kept showing me that real strength often comes when I admit what I can't do. The first time I let my neighbor mow my lawn after surgery, I felt exposed and awkward. Yet, as she finished and sat with me on the porch afterward, something shifted between us. We talked honestly about worry, aging, and faith—a depth of friendship we never shared when I was always the helper. Weakness became a doorway to real connection.

Depending on others can actually be an invitation to deeper relationships and spiritual growth. When you let someone help you, you give them a chance to serve and love in return. You allow humility to take root—a humility that softens your heart and opens your life to grace in new ways. It's not easy at first. Sometimes pride flares up. Sometimes you fear overstepping or losing your voice in decisions that matter. That's why it helps to set boundaries about what kind of help you're comfortable with and to communicate clearly with those around you. You can say "yes" to some offers and "not right now" to others without guilt or resentment.

Saying "thank you" has become one of my spiritual disciplines. When someone carries groceries or sits with me during a tough afternoon, I try not just to mutter a quick thanks but to pause and let gratitude really sink in. That simple act honors both giver and receiver. It's a small way to acknowledge that our lives are always intertwined, no matter our age or abilities. You might try keeping a list of ways you can bless others, even while you're receiving help—praying for caregivers by name, sending notes of encouragement, or sharing wisdom learned from years of experience.

I've met people who built beautiful ministries from places others might call weakness. There's Edna, who moved into a nursing home after her stroke and started a prayer chain with other residents. She couldn't walk far or cook meals anymore, but her room became a hub of encouragement and spiritual support for both staff and neighbors alike. Or Jack, who welcomed regular visits from church friends after a fall left him homebound. Instead of seeing himself as just a recipient, he treated each visit as an opportunity for hospitality—offering stories, prayer, or a listening ear over cups of tea. What looked like loss on the surface became a new way to serve.

If you find yourself struggling with the fear of dependency, consider reframing it as interdependence—a chance to experience community as God meant it to be. None of us were created to do life isolated or self-sufficient forever. Letting others in isn't defeat—it's courage in action. Each time you honestly accept help or offer blessing from your place of need, you mirror the way Christ lived: not above others but right alongside them, sharing both burdens and joys.

These years bring new challenges, yes, but also surprising gifts if we're willing to see them. You might discover your most meaningful connections and deepest spiritual insights not in times of strength but in those moments you invite others into your weakness—and let God's strength shine through both of you.

When Prayer Feels Empty—Navigating Spiritual Dry Spells

Some mornings, I sit with my Bible and coffee, trying to pray, but the words won't come. God can feel far away, making prayer seem like speaking to the ceiling. I used to assume this was my fault or a sign my faith was weak, but it's actually a common experience—especially during life changes, routine disruptions, or after losses. Even faithful figures in Scripture struggled with spiritual dryness. David's psalms express longing and frustration ("How long, O Lord? Will you forget me forever?" Psalm 13:1). Mother Teresa privately shared years of feeling distant from God, despite the inspiration she brought to millions. If your prayers feel empty, know you're not alone; this is part of a real, honest faith journey.

During these dry spells, it helps to keep prayer simple and stick to routines that don't depend on feeling inspired. On some mornings, I just recite the Lord's Prayer slowly or repeat a short verse, like "The Lord is my shepherd." I keep favorite psalms or written prayers nearby for days I have no words—Psalm 23 and Psalm 61 are dependable comforts. On especially tough days, I set a timer for five minutes and sit in silence, telling God I have nothing to say but am present anyway. Often, just showing up takes more faith than fancy words.

Injecting creativity can revive a tired heart. Sometimes I listen to hymns or worship songs, letting the lyrics be my prayers. Other days, a walk outdoors—praying quietly with each step—draws my spirit out of its rut: "Thank you for the sunlight," "Be near to me today," "Help me trust You." If I'm stuck indoors, I'll doodle a verse or color a simple drawing while listening to music. Prayer doesn't always mean folded hands; it can be art, music, or movement—anything that helps you be present with God.

During one particularly numb season of loneliness, I started a "prayer in the darkness" journal. My entries were very short: one sentence about what felt empty, followed by a simple request for God to hold me. Looking back months later, I saw how many small prayers were answered in subtle ways—a call from a friend when I needed it, a sense of peace at night, a laugh over an old photo. At the time, it didn't seem spiritual, but it quietly nurtured my faith beneath the surface.

Others find praying with someone else helps break the silence. A friend of mine and her neighbor prayed together by phone every Thursday for five minutes. Sometimes neither said much, but simply showing up together gradually lightened the heaviness and brought more hope, even if circumstances didn't visibly change.

If you're trudging through a season where God seems remote or your prayers feel hollow, it's okay to admit it. Don't force feelings you don't have or pretend everything is fine. Faith isn't about always feeling inspired—it can mean holding on through routine, honest prayers until the dryness lifts. Use brief, honest prayers or written ones if you struggle for words. Sit quietly and trust God hears even your silence.

Mix up your approach if you need to: listen to worship music, draw or paint as you reflect on a verse, take walks and pray with each step, or jot a daily line in your journal about what feels empty and what you're hoping for. Reach out for a prayer partner—sometimes another person's faith can lift yours when your own feels weak.

Dry spells are often where faith deepens—not because they're pleasant, but because they stretch us to trust God's presence even when we can't sense Him. If you're in such a season, remember: you're not abandoned or broken. Even silence can be sacred when you're willing to wait and keep praying, no matter how simple those prayers may be.

Facing Doubt Without Shame—Biblical Stories for Troubled Hearts

Doubt often creeps in quietly, like a draft under a door. Even during Bible reading, singing hymns, or sitting in church, you can feel nagging questions: "Is God listening?" "Why is my prayer unanswered?" "Am I still loved when I feel uncertain?" This can be unsettling, especially with changing routines and unexpected challenges in retirement. You may long for earlier times when faith felt easy, but now God feels distant, sparking unwarranted shame—"Shouldn't I know better by now?" However, doubt isn't a failure; it's part of being human. Questioning God isn't about lacking faith, but desiring deeper understanding.

Scripture shows we're not alone in this. Think of "Doubting Thomas." Although he spent years with Jesus, he couldn't trust in the resurrection without seeing proof. Jesus didn't scold him; He gently met Thomas's need for reassurance. This reassures my own restless heart. Elijah, despite witnessing miracles, ran for his life in fear and despair, longing to give up. Instead of rebuke, God sent an angel with food and rest, then comforted him in a gentle whisper. John the Baptist, after baptizing Jesus and hearing God's voice, later questioned, "Are you really the One?" in his hardship. His honest doubt didn't erase his faith—it showed genuine wrestling with life's hard questions.

These stories reflect our own struggles. Sometimes faith feels strong; other times, it's delicate. This is especially true during life transitions, loss, unanswered prayers, or aging. The Bible doesn't erase doubt but encourages us to bring our uncertainties into honest dialogue—with God and trusted people who listen without judgment.

For me, writing "doubt letters" to God during sleepless nights became cathartic. I poured out questions like, "Why do you seem silent?" and "Why did things turn out this way?" Initially, I feared these letters meant my faith was weakening. Yet as I wrote, I realized God welcomes my honesty. Just as He never turned away from Thomas, Elijah, or John, God remains present with us in our doubts. If uncertainty weighs on you, try jotting down your questions in a journal. The act of naming your doubts can bring relief.

Talking with others also lightens the load. I meet with a church group where we share our doubts honestly, sometimes leading to deeper fellowship and even laughter over our shared struggles. If you trust someone—a prayer partner, pastor, or friend—consider expressing what's really on your heart. Often, you'll find they're dealing with similar questions.

Practical routines help, too. I keep a journal of God's past faithfulness. When doubt arises, I revisit memories of unexpected comfort or provision—like a timely phone call, medical strength, or a financial answer. These recollections provide a bridge from past assurance to current uncertainty. Listening to or reading about others' struggles with doubt can also encourage—biographies or testimonies remind us that faith and questions coexist.

A helpful practice is keeping a "doubt and hope" list in your journal. On one side, write your specific doubts—"Does God care about my loneliness?" or "Will He provide for my family?" On the other, note moments of hope—comforting verses, memories of God's presence, or small signs of peace. Seeing both side by side reminds me that doubt and hope can exist together in faith.

No one is immune to doubt—not even those with long histories in church or ministry. Doubt does not define your relationship with God; honesty does. Bringing your questions into the open, whether by writing or speaking them, leads to deeper understanding and trust—even if not every question is answered. Faith isn't the absence of doubt, but the practice of returning to the One who welcomes your whole self—questions included—with open arms.

Cultivating Blessed Assurance—Practices for Resting in God's Faithfulness

There's a special peace that settles in when you truly know you're safe in God's hands—what many call "blessed assurance." It isn't about having all the answers or never feeling anxious; it's a steady confidence that, despite life's uncertainties, God is faithful, loving, and present. For me, singing the hymn "Blessed Assurance" as a retiree made these words—"This is my story, this is my song"—feel deeper and more personal. It became a declaration over my life, past and future, that my story is anchored in Jesus, not in my own strength.

Embracing Assurance in Retirement

In retirement, when routines and sources of confidence change, blessed assurance becomes vital. It's easy to get caught up in regrets or worries, but assurance brings you back to the present, reminding you that "God has never failed you yet." Surrounding yourself with reminders of God's faithfulness helps nurture this assurance. I began singing hymns or reciting them each morning—imperfectly, but sincerely. Even humming "Great Is Thy Faithfulness" during chores can turn a mundane moment into a quiet prayer. Keeping scripture verses about God's love and security nearby—taped to a mirror or near your chair—can ground you. When anxiety comes at night, verses like Isaiah 43:1—"Fear not, for I have redeemed you; I have called you by name; you are mine"—bring comfort.

Practical Ways to Remember

Another grounding practice is maintaining a "God's faithfulness" journal. Whenever I notice a prayer answered, a worry eased, or a simple blessing—like a call from a friend—I jot it down. Over time, these notes create a record of God's goodness to revisit during tough times. Some friends use affirmation cards or frame verses at home as visual cues, anchoring themselves and visitors in God's love. These reminders are more than decorations; they offer stability during shaky days.

Sharing stories of God's faithfulness also strengthens assurance. Family gatherings, Bible studies, or legacy letters to loved ones are great opportunities to recount times when God provided or comforted you. You don't need fancy words; honest, heartfelt stories encourage hope in others and yourself.

Living Out Assurance

Resting in assurance transforms daily life. You're freed from measuring your worth by productivity or physical ability, and joy returns when you focus on what God has already done. I've seen anxious retirees find new energy after turning their attention to God's promises instead of their problems. One friend posted verses on her fridge and sang hymns at breakfast, finding more encouragement than she ever got from the news. Another shared brief testimonies at her church, uplifting others facing similar struggles.

Simple Steps to Build Confidence

To develop this confidence, start small. Pick a hymn or verse to memorize and repeat it during daily routines—laundry, walks, or waiting at appointments. Begin journaling answered prayers and blessings. Place reminders where you'll see them often, like a favorite psalm on your nightstand, affirmation cards in your wallet, or hymn lyrics by your door.

There's no secret formula for resting in God's faithfulness; it grows through simple, daily habits and actively celebrating His goodness. The more you repeat these truths, the more naturally you'll rest in them, even amid troubles.

Stepping Stones Toward Peace

As these practices become habits, you may notice anxiety fading and peace taking root. Blessed assurance isn't reserved for hymnals or Sunday mornings—it's for any day you wake up uncertain but still choose to trust.

In closing, remember assurance comes not from perfect faith, but persistent trust in a faithful God. Singing truth, journaling blessings, and sharing stories become stepping stones to deeper peace. As you move forward into building family bonds and legacies, bring this sense of security with you, letting it shape how you love and approach each new day—with hope, not worry.

Chapter 7
Strengthening Family Bonds

Grandparenting as Kingdom Work—Creative Faith-Building Ideas

"Tell it to your children, and let your children tell it to their children, and their children to the next generation."
— *Joel 1:3 (NIV)*

I once believed that grandparenting was a reward—a chance to spoil little ones and enjoy the fun without the full-time responsibility. But over time, I've come to see it as something far more sacred. It's Kingdom work.

Joel 1:3 calls us to pass down the stories of God's faithfulness—not just to our children, but to our children's children.

That means my role isn't just to bake cookies or babysit (though I do love both!). My role is to plant seeds of faith, to model love, and to speak truth into young hearts that are still learning who they are. Sometimes it's reading a Bible story before bed. Sometimes it's a quiet prayer whispered over a sleeping grandchild. Sometimes it's simply living in a way that shows what trusting Jesus looks like in real life.

The world may be changing fast, but God's truth is unshakable. And if I can help anchor the next generation in that truth—even in small, creative ways—then I've done something eternal.

I never expected that the most meaningful purpose of my later years would be investing in my grandkids—but these moments are lasting in ways no job or project ever was. The smallest everyday activities—reading a story, sending a postcard, gardening together—can be sacred opportunities for faith to take root. Grandparenting isn't just something extra; it's a calling. Even if you lack the energy of youth, your experience, patience, and wisdom are needed now more than ever.

Scripture gives a beautiful example of spiritual grandparenting in Lois and Eunice. Though their appearances in the New Testament are brief, their legacy is powerful: Lois' sincere faith influenced her daughter Eunice, who then raised Timothy in faith—and Paul saw their influence as the foundation for Timothy's ministry (see 2 Timothy 1:5). They didn't preach grand sermons, but their consistent, loving, everyday modeling of faith shaped generations. Our simple choices, prayers, and words can echo much further than we realize

(Who Were Lois and Eunice in the Bible?).

There are gentle, creative ways to nurture faith in grandkids of any age or personality. For young children, games and crafts are natural openings for spiritual conversation. Try "Bible charades," act out favorite stories, or make simple scripture-related crafts—such as rainbow mobiles after Noah's story or paper doves when discussing peace. Baking together allows for meaningful talks; as you knead dough, share how Jesus is the "Bread of Life" and how God provides for our needs. Planting seeds together offers a tangible way to discuss how faith grows—sometimes slow, sometimes blooming suddenly.

Storytelling is especially powerful. Both children and teens love hearing true stories, especially from trusted family.

Share times God answered your prayers, helped you through difficulties, or brought you joy. These don't need to be dramatic—often, it's the ordinary stories that stick. If you need a conversation starter, ask your grandchild about their current concerns or hopes, then share a memory where you faced something similar and saw God at work.

Long-distance grandparenting can still be spiritually rich. Some grandparents send regular postcards with handwritten Bible verses, prayers, or cheerful doodles. Mailing small devotionals or faith-based books is another way to connect—inscribe a short, loving note inside for a personal touch. Use technology for video calls: read Bible stories together or pray before bed. Some families hold "Faith Fridays" on Zoom to share weekly highs and lows before a short devotion or song.

If your adult children aren't believers or feel uneasy with spiritual conversations for their kids, be gentle and respectful. The best witness is a steady, Christlike love—be patient, supportive, and a good listener. Avoid pressure or preaching; always ask before sharing faith resources. If permitted, keep it subtle—a picture book, a short prayer. If not, let your caring actions and encouragement speak for themselves.

Interactive Element: Faith-Building Grandparenting Checklist

- Share one Bible story or answered prayer from your life with your grandchild this month.
- Plan a simple activity like baking together or planting seeds while gently weaving in faith.

- Mail a postcard with an encouraging Bible verse or blessing.
- Try video storytime or prayer, even for just five minutes.
- Reflect: Am I living out Christlike love in my words and actions?
- For grandchildren whose parents aren't believers, always check with their parents before sharing spiritual resources.

Whether your grandkids live nearby or far away, whether they're toddlers or teens, your influence is profound. Results may not appear right away—sometimes faith grows quietly beneath the surface—but every small act of love and faith matters. The seeds you plant now may someday be the roots that help your family weather storms you can't even foresee.

Blessings and Prayers for the Next Generation

There's a unique power in spoken blessings. Words of blessing linger in the air and settle on the heart, carrying a gentle, holy weight. The first time I blessed my grandchild—placing my hand on her shoulder and speaking words of hope before her new school year—I realized how meaningful and sacred those moments could be. These aren't just wishes; they invite God's presence and anchor our loved ones in faith. Blessing is a living tradition for all ages and relationships.

Throughout Scripture, blessings move from one generation to the next. When Jacob blessed his grandsons Ephraim and Manasseh (Genesis 48), it was no casual farewell. His intentional words became a spiritual inheritance, remembered by the family and shaping the boys' sense of identity. Such blessings are more than prayers—they connect our loved ones to a greater spiritual story.

Blessings needn't be grand or poetic; sincerity is enough. They can be spoken aloud, written in a card, whispered at bedtime, or even texted. A simple line in a birthday card—"May the Lord bless you with wisdom, courage, and His peace this year"—has an impact. For major milestones like graduations or weddings, tailor the words: "As you enter this new chapter, may God guide you and give you strength." Seasonal transitions, like a new school year, are perfect times for a brief blessing: "May God surround you with good friends and help you shine His light." Any small, heartfelt note or message can leave a lasting imprint.

When writing your own blessing, focus on what you hope to see grow in your grandchild—kindness, faith, resilience—and pair it with a scriptural promise or simple prayer. Personal touches help make blessings memorable: "May God fill your heart with compassion and grant you peace when life feels hard." Or, "May you always know you are loved—not only by me but by your Heavenly Father." Specific details that reflect your unique relationship make it even more meaningful.

Prayer and blessing go together. I keep a small journal, one page per grandchild, where I write down prayers: "Give Ellie confidence today," or "Help Ben make wise choices." Over time, this journal fills with hopes and gratitude, each answered prayer marked with a date. I occasionally share pages with my grandkids or their parents—it's a faith keepsake. If writing isn't your strength, try recording your prayers and sending audio clips. Even if met with eye-rolls now, these prayers might become treasures in their future.

Making blessings a family affair turns them into treasured traditions. At reunions or holidays, we sometimes use a "blessing bowl"—each person writes a short encouraging note, drops it in, and we read them aloud. Though awkward at first, it's become a favorite ritual—children blessing grandparents, cousins blessing each other. On special days like birthdays, gathering to lay hands on and pray for someone as a group creates closeness and lasting memories.

To adopt these rituals, start simply. Offer a brief prayer at meals or bedtime. Slip a written blessing into a card or backpack before big events.

Invite others to share in giving blessings at family gatherings. There's no perfect formula—only the intention and love behind your words matter.

Blessing Templates for Everyday Moments

- Birthday: "May God fill your year with laughter, learning, and true friends."
- Graduation: "As you begin this adventure, may God give you wisdom and guide your steps."
- New School Year: "May you walk in courage and kindness; may God's presence go before you."
- Everyday: "May God's peace guard your heart today."

Blessings and prayers don't require ornate words or training—just your willingness to speak hope and pass on faith. Trust that these simple words will linger in your loved ones' hearts long after you say them.

Navigating Shifting Roles With Adult Children

"Train up a child in the way he should go; even when he is old he will not depart from it."
— *Proverbs 22:6 (ESV)*

Letting go is one of the hardest things I've had to learn as a parent. When my children were little, they needed me for everything—from tying shoes to making decisions. But now they're adults, and I find myself in unfamiliar territory: wanting to guide, but needing to step back; wanting to protect, but knowing it's no longer my place.

Proverbs 22:6 reminds me that my role was never to control their path, but to prepare them for it. I poured into them the best I could—faith, values, love—and now I must trust that those seeds will take root in God's perfect timing.

My role isn't over—it's just different. Now I listen more than I instruct. I pray more than I plan. And I cheer them on from a quiet place, confident that what God began in them, He will carry through. It sneaks up on you—the gradual change as your children become adults, create their own families, homes, and opinions. The nature of your relationship shifts: phone calls are different, holidays feel unfamiliar, and suddenly you aren't in charge of appointments or their social circles. You might hesitate to give advice, unsure whether to speak up or simply listen. I remember the first time my eldest said, "Dad, we've got it covered." I felt proud but also a small ache from not being needed in the same way. It's a unique challenge—letting go but wanting to stay close, supporting without interfering.

Letting go of control doesn't mean ending the relationship; it means evolving from director to companion. Trusting your children as adults, even when you don't understand their choices, is key. When my son and his wife made decisions I didn't expect, I had to remind myself to respect their autonomy. I often pray for wisdom to know when to speak, when to step back, and how to offer support without taking over. The urge to help or guide never completely goes away, but real support is about being present, steady, and loving—regardless of the outcome.

Communication with adult children can be delicate, especially during disagreements. I've learned that active listening makes a difference. Instead of immediately offering solutions, I try to really hear what they're saying—listening not just for the words but the feelings beneath. Sometimes I'll reflect back: "It sounds like you're overwhelmed at work," or, "You'd like to handle this your way." This simple act can defuse tension and show I respect their perspective. When I want to give advice, I ask first: "Would you like my thoughts on this?" Sometimes they say yes; sometimes they only want to vent. Respecting their preference helps keep trust intact.

Boundaries also become important, particularly with financial help or in crises. If you're able to assist, set clear, compassionate guidelines. Before offering money or moving in after the arrival of a baby, talk openly about expectations—how long you'll help, and what the plan is if things change. Sorting these details together avoids misunderstandings later. If you need support with errands or medical care, be honest about your needs and agree on routines that work for everyone. Holidays can also require negotiation—alternate hosting, blend gatherings, or start fresh traditions that suit this new stage.

Differences in parenting or faith practices can feel sensitive. If your children raise their kids differently or don't share your spiritual habits, disappointment or worry is common. But your grown children are responsible for their own choices. Your role is to respect their decisions and show grace, not pressure or criticize. This doesn't mean you never express your values; it means you do so with humility and warmth, not as a demand but as an invitation.

Blessing your adult children can be hard if there's conflict or distance.

Sometimes, when speaking is difficult, writing a letter helps. A note of honest affirmation can bridge gaps spoken words cannot. Say you're proud of them and grateful for their presence, even if you disagree. Find something genuine to celebrate about their lives. If reconciliation seems impossible for now, prayer is an anchor—lifting them up to God and asking for peace and healing. Sometimes, loving from a distance and trusting God's unseen work is all you can do.

Navigating these changing roles isn't easy—it's a process that challenges us to grow just as much as our children do. There's beauty in learning how to love your adult kids as they are now—not as you remember or wish, but as unique individuals making their own way through life's ups and downs. Every act of grace—listening, setting boundaries, or quietly praying—nourishes your relationship, even in difficult seasons.

Sharing Your Testimony—Storytelling as Spiritual Heritage

Stories have a mysterious way of sticking, far longer than rules or advice. I think back to evenings when my grandmother would sit, hands folded, and tell us about the times she saw God work in ways that seemed impossible. Those quiet stories—often shared after supper, sometimes while washing dishes—are still with me, shaping how I see faith and hope. Personal stories aren't just entertainment; they leave a mark, passing values and faith from one generation to the next. Moses once told the Israelites to recount to their children all that God had done for them (Deuteronomy 6). He knew that stories are memory's anchor, tying our hearts to the truth of God's faithfulness.

You don't need to be a polished speaker or a writer with perfect grammar. Your testimony is valuable just as it is, honest and real. Maybe you wonder where to start or worry that your faith story is too ordinary. The truth is, ordinary stories are often what our families need most. Begin by mapping out a simple "faith timeline." List out the major moments—when you first sensed God's presence, times of difficulty when faith was tested, unexpected answers to prayer. Include moments of doubt or struggle; these often become the most meaningful parts of your story. Writing it down can help clarify what you want to share. I keep a small notebook where I jot down memories as they come—sometimes triggered by a hymn on the radio or the smell of fresh bread.

Choosing which stories to tell matters too. Focus on those that reveal God's presence in hardship or uncertainty. Maybe it was the loss of a job, an illness, or a season of loneliness when God met you in quiet ways. These stories show your family that faith isn't about having everything together; it's about finding hope and peace even when life is difficult. Sometimes, sharing how you handled disappointment or made mistakes—and how God met you there—will connect more than tales of success.

One of my favorite ways to pass down faith is through music. Sharing a hymn that has comforted me—explaining why "Great Is Thy Faithfulness" or "How Great Thou Art" means so much—opens up conversations that lectures never could. I've noticed that music jogs memories across generations, and sometimes singing together leads to unexpected sharing: "Tell me about a time when God felt close to you?" Suddenly, you're not just telling a story, but inviting others into it.

Modern life gives us creative tools for preserving testimony. Recording your story as an audio message or a short video can make your voice last long after you're gone. Don't worry about production quality—just speak from the heart. Some families make this part of their holiday gatherings: everyone shares a memory or lesson from the past year, and someone records them all. These become treasures for grandchildren and great-grandchildren. If you keep scrapbooks or family photo albums, tuck in handwritten notes about what God did during certain seasons—maybe next to a wedding picture or a snapshot from a family reunion. Even a simple caption like, "We prayed for this home for years," gives context that photos alone can't provide.

Honest storytelling is more powerful than perfection. Don't shy away from sharing struggles with doubt or moments when you felt far from God. These stories remind your family that faith is not a straight line but a winding path with ups and downs. My grandchildren have asked tough questions: "Did you ever doubt God?" "Were you scared during surgery?" I try not to sugarcoat my answers. I talk about sleepless nights and prayers that felt unanswered at first—and then the slow, surprising ways God brought comfort or change. This vulnerability opens doors for deeper conversations and trust.

Invite your family members to ask questions about your experiences. Sometimes children and teens want to know what life was like when you were their age, or how you handled things like bullying, heartbreak, or fear. Answer honestly—even if your story includes mistakes or regret. Tell them how God led you through those moments, what you learned, and how you found hope again.

Reflection Section: Testimony Timeline Exercise

Take some quiet time to sketch your "faith timeline." Draw a line on paper and mark significant spiritual moments—first encounters with God, times of loss, answered prayers, seasons of doubt, and moments of renewal. Next to each event, write a sentence or two describing what happened and how you saw God at work (or what you wrestled with). Use this timeline as a guide for sharing stories with your family—one at a time, as opportunities arise.

The act of sharing your testimony isn't about boasting or trying to impress your family; it's about handing them a piece of your heart—a living heritage of faith that can steady them in their own storms someday. The stories you tell today may become the foundation your loved ones stand on long after you're gone.

Building Family Devotional Traditions

Family devotional time doesn't need to look like a church service at the dining room table. I used to believe devotions had to be lengthy or led by someone with deep biblical knowledge, but that's not true. The most meaningful moments often happen when a family simply sits together, opens a Bible, and shares even a few honest words or prayers. Finding a time that works for everyone is half the battle—sometimes it's breakfast, other times it's just before bed. In my family, it has changed with every season. When grandkids were small, we'd gather after supper, sometimes right in the middle of toy chaos and spilled juice. Now, with teens and busy schedules, it might be a Sunday evening or even a quick check-in over the phone. The key is flexibility and willingness, not perfection.

One way to make devotions come alive across generations is by weaving in activities that engage different ages. Family prayer walks—wandering the neighborhood, pausing to pray for neighbors or thank God for flowers and birds—bring everyone outside and get bodies moving, making it less formal and more natural. Another simple idea is creating a "faith jar." Fill a jar with slips of paper—each bearing a scripture, prayer prompt, or question ("What's something you're grateful for today?"). Once a week, someone pulls out a slip, reads it aloud, and the family discusses or prays together. This works well around the dinner table or even virtually if your family is spread out. I've seen kids light up at the chance to pick from the jar or add their own ideas.

Storytime has always been a favorite in our house. Reading Bible stories aloud—whether from a children's Bible or straight from scripture—opens space for real conversation. Afterward, I like to ask open-ended questions: "What would you have done in that story?" or "How do you see God at work here?" There's no right answer, and sometimes the youngest voices have the most surprising insights. Mixing in discussion keeps everyone engaged. For older kids or adults, focusing on passages that connect to current family situations—like forgiveness after a disagreement or trusting God during a tough time—makes scripture feel relevant.

Variety is vital to holding attention. Rotating leadership can help; one week, Grandma leads with her favorite psalm, another week a teenager might pick a worship song or share a short reading. Including music shifts the mood—singing together or even just listening to a hymn softens hearts and pulls people together. Some families add hands-on elements: drawing pictures inspired by the story, acting out scenes, or building something that connects to the theme (like making paper boats after reading about Jesus calming the storm). These activities aren't just for kids; adults often rediscover joy and creativity alongside their younger relatives.

Art also bridges gaps—try having everyone create something during devotions. Paint rocks with encouraging words from scripture and place them in the yard or around town for others to find. Create a family gratitude poster where each person adds blessings throughout the week. These visual reminders can linger long after the devotional time ends.

Of course, obstacles arise. Busy schedules collide, attention wavers, and households sometimes hold a mix of beliefs, making devotional time feel tense or awkward. I've learned that keeping devotions short and flexible removes pressure. Even five minutes of shared prayer or reflection counts. If someone prefers to listen rather than speak, that's perfectly fine—invite participation but never force it. For families with varied spiritual backgrounds, focus on universal themes like gratitude, kindness, or hope. Use stories that highlight values everyone can appreciate and offer optional faith-based reflections for those who want them.

Allowing for messiness and interruption goes a long way. Don't expect every session to run smoothly; sometimes kids will argue, phones will buzz, or someone will be called away unexpectedly. Laughter and patience are part of the process. What matters is the regular rhythm of coming together—however imperfectly—and making space for God's presence in your home.

Visual Element: Sample "Faith Jar" Prompts

- "Share one thing you're thankful for this week."
- "Read Psalm 23 aloud—where do you feel God's comfort right now?"
- "Tell about a time you helped someone."
- "Pray for someone outside our family."
- "What's one worry you want to give to God today?"

Devotional traditions are less about structure and more about connection—both with each other and with God. Adapting as you go and keeping an open heart will help your family build faith memories that last through every season of life.

"Passing the Baton"—Encouraging Faith in Moments of Transition

There's something about those big life changes that makes you stop and pay attention. You can feel it when graduation sneaks up, when a child packs up for college, or when a grandchild says "I do" at the altar. Even in retirement, that sense of standing on the edge of something new is so real it almost tingles in your bones. These transitions aren't just milestones; they hold a kind of holy potential—a chance to speak into the lives of those you love, to nudge the next chapter forward with hope and faith. I've come to realize that these moments are some of the most powerful opportunities we have to encourage and bless our families.

The Bible paints a vivid picture of this with Paul and Timothy. Paul often wrote about running the race well, but he also spoke of handing off the baton—passing on wisdom, faith, and responsibility to those coming after him. In his letters, Paul encouraged Timothy not just with teaching but with deep affirmation: "Don't let anyone look down on you because you are young." That trust, that blessing, set Timothy free to take his place in ministry. It's a powerful metaphor—one person stretching out their hand, baton in palm, trusting the next runner to take it and keep going.

You don't need a stage or a spotlight to do something similar in your own family. Simple rituals can turn an ordinary day into a spiritual marker. At graduations, I like to give a family Bible—sometimes the one I've marked up over the years, other times a new one with a handwritten message tucked inside. It's not about the book itself, but about saying, "Here's what has guided me—may it guide you." Before big moves or marriages, I try to gather everyone for a moment of prayer. Sometimes it's awkward, sometimes tears flow, but always there's a sense that God is near, listening as we release our loved ones into whatever comes next.

One tradition that has brought unexpected closeness is writing "legacy letters." When someone in the family faces a major change, we gather for an evening—phones put away—and write short notes about our hopes for each other's future. These aren't essays; just honest words about faith, values, or lessons learned through mistakes and grace. Reading them aloud can be emotional. I remember one grandson saying quietly after hearing his mother's letter, "I didn't know you felt that way." These letters become keepsakes long after the event passes.

Conversations about faith and values shouldn't wait until the moving truck is packed or the wedding reception ends. I've found it helps to be proactive. Share your hopes for how faith might stay alive in your family—not as a lecture but as a gentle invitation. Ask your loved ones what questions or dreams they have when it comes to God or life's meaning. Sometimes they surprise you with honesty; sometimes they shrug it off. Either way, you've opened a door for real talk down the road.

Stepping back doesn't mean disappearing. After big transitions, my role has often shifted from active guide to faithful supporter on the sidelines. I keep praying for my kids and grandkids, even when I don't know all the details of their lives anymore. A text message or card with encouragement goes further than you might think—"I'm still cheering you on." When I see one of my children step up to lead prayer at a family meal or offer advice to a sibling, I try to celebrate it openly: "Look at how you're leading now." It's good to recognize when it's time for the next generation to take the baton while still letting them know you have their back.

Transitions will always come—some welcome, others painful or unexpected. Each is an invitation to bless, encourage, and remind those we love that they carry not just our hopes but God's promise into their new season. Whether you mark these moments with ceremony or quiet blessing, what matters most is your presence, your prayers, and your willingness to trust God with what comes next.

Looking back at this chapter, it's clear that faith isn't just spoken—it's handed on through intentional words, small rituals, honest conversations, and our steady support during life's turning points. Every transition becomes another chance to encourage courage and hope in those we love. In the chapters ahead, we'll explore how daily choices—big and small—can fill your later years with purpose and joy that lasts beyond any single milestone.

Chapter 8 Living Each Day With Meaning, Joy, and Hope

Practicing Presence—Finding God in the Ordinary

"In him we live and move and have our being."
— *Acts 17:28a (NIV)*

For much of my life, I looked for God in the big moments—worship services, answered prayers, mountaintop experiences. But now, in this quieter season, I'm learning to find Him in the small things: the warm cup of tea, the birdsong outside my window, the slow rhythm of a daily walk.

Acts 17:28 reminds me that I don't have to chase after God—He's already here. *In Him we live and move and have our being.* That means He's in the doing of the dishes, in the laughter of a grandchild, in the silence of a morning devotional.

Each day, no matter how ordinary, becomes extraordinary when I live it with awareness. Practicing presence isn't about doing more—it's about noticing more. And when I do, I find joy. I find meaning. I find hope. Because I find Him.

It's funny how life can surprise you with meaning when you least expect it. One morning, not so long ago, I found myself in the kitchen, scrubbing a stubborn spot on a plate. Sunlight spilled across the counter, catching the steam from the sink and turning it into a kind of golden mist. For a moment, I stopped what I was doing and just watched. There was nothing grand about that plate or the soap bubbles. Yet, right there, I felt God whisper to my heart—"I'm here too." It struck me how easy it is to overlook Him in daily routines. We wait for big moments or special occasions, but God doesn't. He meets us in the ordinary, in the middle of dishes, laundry, or a morning walk.

You might not realize how often God tries to get your attention through simple things. Take a look outside during your next stroll—notice how the birds hop from branch to branch, each one chirping in its own rhythm. The breeze brushing your cheek, the pattern of sunlight on leaves, even the hum of distant traffic can become reminders of His nearness if you allow yourself to notice. Sometimes I catch myself grumbling about a stiff knee as I walk up the driveway, but when I pause and listen to a robin's song or see dew sparkling in the grass, I remember I am not alone. Even pulling weeds or watering tomatoes can become holy moments if you invite Jesus into them—thanking Him for ripe fruit or laughing at a worm wriggling through the soil.

Let's talk about practical ways to turn these small windows of time into something more sacred. Mealtime isn't just about eating—try saying a quiet prayer of gratitude before your first bite, even if you're alone at the table. When you're gardening, let each planted seed remind you of God's faithfulness to bring new life out of hidden places. Waiting for the coffee to brew? That's another chance to breathe deep and whisper thanks for another day. Right before you pick up the phone or head into an appointment, pause for a moment of silent reflection—ask God for peace or kind words. These small pauses add up; they build a habit of inviting Christ into your daily routines.

There's a practice called "holy attentiveness" that might sound fancy but is really just about paying close attention on purpose. Begin with your senses—close your eyes and listen for God's voice in birdsong, the laughter of someone you love, or even your own quiet breathing. Smell the bread baking or the fresh-cut grass and let it become a prayer of thanksgiving. Try journaling your "God sightings" at the end of each day—noticing where you sensed His presence or received an unexpected kindness. Maybe you heard an old hymn on the radio that brought back good memories, or maybe it was a stranger's smile at the grocery store that made your heart lighter.

I've met folks who found God in the most unlikely settings. My friend Doris once told me about waiting at her doctor's office, nervous about test results. She started watching people come and go—some anxious, some cheerful—and decided to pray quietly for each person she saw. By the time her name was called, her own fear had eased, replaced by an odd sense of peace. Another neighbor shared how folding laundry became her prayer time—she'd pray for each family member as she paired their socks or folded shirts. Sometimes God speaks in these repetitive tasks, nudging us to remember loved ones and offer them up in prayer.

I remember a quiet afternoon when rain pattered against the windows and I sat with my Bible open but couldn't focus on the words. Instead, I gazed outside and simply said, "Lord, are You here?" In that silence, I felt comforted—a sense that even on uneventful days, God listens and responds in His own gentle ways.

Interactive Element: Reflection Exercise—Journaling Your "God Sightings"

Take a few minutes each evening this week to jot down three moments when you noticed God's presence or felt extra thankful during your day. Maybe it was a beautiful view from your window, the scent of dinner cooking, a good conversation, or even a quiet moment of rest. Don't worry about sounding poetic—just be honest and specific. Over time, you'll start to see how often God shows up in places you once overlooked.

There's no need for grand gestures or perfect prayers here. The goal isn't to impress but simply to notice—to let

God transform ordinary minutes into sacred encounters. You might just find that joy and hope sneak up on you while doing something as simple as washing dishes or tying your shoes.

Embracing the Slow Pace—Sabbath Rest and Renewal

"Come to me, all you who are weary and burdened, and I will give you rest."
— *Matthew 11:28 (NIV)*

There's something almost countercultural about slowing down these days. Everyone seems to be rushing from one commitment to another, as if busy-ness is a badge of honor. Yet, if you look back at Genesis, God set a different rhythm for us. On the seventh day, after creating everything from the stars to the tiniest seed, He stopped. He didn't stop because He was tired—He was showing us how to enjoy His creation and simply be. That invitation to Sabbath, to pause and rest, is still open for you and me. It's not just about doing nothing; it's about making room for renewal, for letting your soul breathe and remember who holds it all together.

In retirement, you might find that the pace of life changes whether you planned for it or not. The calendar isn't as packed, but that empty space can feel just as restless as a full one. I remember one Sunday afternoon when I decided not to schedule anything at all. No errands, no chores, no social obligations. I sat with a cup of tea by the window and just watched the clouds move across the sky. It was quiet, almost alarmingly so at first. Yet as I settled in, I felt a gentle peace wash over me—a sense that God was delighted I'd finally stopped running and simply sat with Him. You don't have to wait for everything to be perfect to claim this kind of rest. Setting aside even an hour or two each week can make a difference. You might carve out Sunday afternoons for quiet reflection, or decide that on Tuesdays, no errands will clutter your day.

It's easy to think that rest is only for those who are worn out, but Sabbath invites everyone—active or not—to slow down and receive. If you're looking for ways to make rest more than just an absence of activity, consider creating little rituals that feel special to you. Maybe you open a favorite devotional or thumb through a book of poetry under a cozy blanket. Some folks I know love to linger over slow meals with family or friends, sharing laughter and stories without any hurry to clear the table. Others put on worship music and let it fill the house while they rest in a sunlit room. These aren't extravagant gestures; they're simply ways to mark time as holy, a reminder that God meets you right where you are.

One of the hurdles many face is guilt—the nagging sense that sitting still is lazy or even wasteful. You may catch yourself thinking, "Shouldn't I be doing something useful?" But God delights in your rest just as much as your service. Psalm 23 paints such a clear picture: "He makes me lie down in green pastures." Notice it doesn't say He asks or suggests—it says He makes us pause, as if He knows we'll try to wiggle out of it. There's wisdom in surrendering to moments of stillness. Rest isn't earned; it's given. You don't need to prove your worth by checking off a list of tasks. Sometimes the holiest thing you can do is let yourself be.

To help remind yourself of this truth, try writing a "Sabbath permission slip." Grab a notepad and write out: "I give myself permission to rest today—no guilt, no apologies." Tuck it in your Bible or tape it to the fridge. When the urge to "do more" creeps in, let those words reassure you that God Himself has invited you into rest. Sabbath is about trust—not just in God's ability to run the world without your help for a day, but in His deep care for your well-being.

Renewal often sneaks in through these pauses. When you slow down enough to listen—really listen—you'll start noticing things you missed before: the distant sound of laughter from children playing outside, the warmth of sunlight on your skin, or even just the rise and fall of your own breath as you sit quietly. These moments restore something deep inside. You might discover creative ideas bubbling up during these restful spaces or find old worries losing their grip as you hand them over to God.

Creating intentional rhythms of rest doesn't require perfection or rigid rules. The goal isn't to add another chore but to receive Sabbath as a gift—a gentle invitation to enjoy God's presence, savor life's simple pleasures, and emerge refreshed for whatever comes next.

Finding Joy When Loved Ones Are Gone

"Those who sow with tears will reap with songs of joy."
— *Psalm 126:5 (NIV)*

There are days when the ache of missing them feels sharper than others—when a photo catches me off guard, or a favorite song fills the quiet with memory. For a while, I wondered if joy would ever feel real again. It seemed wrong to laugh, to celebrate, to move forward while carrying such deep loss.

But Psalm 126:5 speaks hope into that tender space: *"Those who sow with tears will reap with songs of joy."* Grief doesn't mean joy is gone forever—it means we're planting something sacred through our sorrow. And in time, God promises that joy will bloom again.

It may come softly—a warm memory, a gentle smile, a moment of peace that feels like a hug from heaven. It's not about forgetting. It's about trusting that God still has beauty to give us, even after deep loss. Our tears are not wasted. They are the beginning of something new.

Nothing really prepares you for how silence settles in when someone dear is gone. The ache colors daily routines—setting one plate, passing an empty chair, hearing a laugh in memory. Anniversaries and birthdays bring a fresh wave of missing. These days can feel so heavy that joy seems unreachable or out of place. My first anniversary after losing my wife was like standing still while the world turned, balancing gratitude for what had been with sorrow for what was lost. Honoring both is a strange challenge.

Grief doesn't respect tidy timelines or neat stages. Some mornings, it lets you breathe; other times, it comes in hard, even years later. Honoring grief isn't weakness. It's love with nowhere to go—all those stories and habits that infused daily life. Over time, though, those deep spaces carved out by loss can hold new sources of light. It's possible to seek joy again, without denying the importance of what was lost.

One practice I started was listing three small things each day that made me smile—a warm cup of tea, a grandchild's joke, comfortable old slippers. This gratitude journal didn't erase pain, but softened it by nudging my attention upward. At first, it felt artificial, but eventually those notes became a lifeline. Small moments of delight help joy return, no matter how fragile.

Laughter may feel forbidden after a major loss, but it's necessary medicine. I found safe spaces to laugh again, like a weekly game night at church with friends who understood if I needed a break or quiet. Sometimes laughter bubbled up unexpectedly—a funny story from an old friend or a child's perfect joke. Laughter doesn't erase grief; it sits alongside it, a reminder that life continues.

Building new traditions can help fill the emptiness. After my best friend died, I joined a community art class. Though I'd never painted before, the focus on mixing colors and watching shapes appear helped distract from sorrow, if only briefly. Others find comfort in gardening clubs, book circles, or even by caring for pets—a neighbor rescued an old beagle and says he rescued her as much as she did him. Healing often comes from caring for someone or something else, finding meaning in these new connections.

I met Alice at a gardening group. Widowed after fifty years, she drifted through gray days after her husband's funeral. She started coming just to get out of the house but stayed because the group, swapping gardening tips and stories, gave her something to anticipate. She told me her first genuine laugh came when a dog chased a squirrel through her flowers, messing up her careful rows. That small, silly disruption was her permission to smile again.

Volunteering gave new meaning to my friend Margaret. For years, she cooked meals for her church during times of illness or grief. After losing her own partner, she returned to volunteering, having experienced firsthand how much comfort a home-cooked casserole could give. Serving others didn't erase the void, but it built a bridge over it, her hands busy with kindness and her heart rediscovering purpose.

Mentoring brought unexpected joy to Jim, a widower who began helping at an after-school program. He simply listened to kids read and shared his own stories. Called "Grandpa Jim," he found himself energized by their laughter. Being needed gave him purpose and, as he says, those afternoons helped him as much as he helped the kids.

Joy after loss looks different than before—quieter, sometimes fragile, but no less real. You don't have to rush or mask sadness to make space for it. Sometimes it slips in through shared memories at gatherings or the first harvest from a solo-planted garden. It may turn up at a craft table, or with a rescue pup who drags you for a walk whatever the weather. Grief and joy can live side by side. You honor loved ones not by forgetting them, but by carrying their spark.

Prayer for Joy in the Midst of Grief

Lord,

You see the tears I still cry and the silence that follows memories too deep for words.

Thank You for walking with me through this grief—not rushing me, not leaving me, but holding me through every wave of sorrow.

Today, I offer You my broken heart, trusting that even in this pain, You are planting something new. Help me believe that joy will return—not in place of my love for them, but because of it.

Let joy and sorrow live side by side in me, making room for laughter again without guilt, for light again without fear.

Thank You for the promise that those who sow in tears will reap with songs of joy.
Give me the courage to hope, the grace to rest, and the eyes to see beauty even in the midst of loss. And when I smile again, let it be a sign of Your healing.

In Jesus' name,
Amen.

Looking Forward—A Heavenly Perspective on Aging

There's something that changes inside when you start seeing the future through the lens of God's promises. I remember, not long after my retirement, sitting with my Bible open to passages about resurrection and eternal life—John 14, 1 Corinthians 15, Paul's words echoing hope. The aches and pains of getting older, the things that used to spark worry about decline or lost time, started to look a little different. I realized, this isn't just the last chapter. It's a prelude to something even better. The wrinkles, the slower steps, the thinning hair—they're not the whole story. They're reminders that there's a forever waiting, one that God Himself has promised.

Aging has a way of making you face things you'd rather avoid. You might find yourself thinking about what comes next—sometimes at 2 a.m., when sleep just won't come. Fears creep in: Will I lose more independence? Will I have the strength to face what's ahead? When these questions get heavy, I've found comfort in writing them down in a letter to God. Sometimes I'll pour out my worries and hopes on paper, not holding anything back. It's a simple practice, but it gives a sense of release—almost like handing over a weight I was never meant to carry alone.

Hope in heaven changes how you see these struggles. The promise that Jesus is preparing a place for us (John 14:2) steadies the heart in ways nothing else can. When my body groans or my mind grows tired, I remind myself: this isn't forever. There's a deeper story unfolding, and God is weaving it with threads I can't always see. Praying for a longing for Christ's return is not about wishing away today—it's about letting hope grow stronger than fear. I've whispered prayers like, "Lord, give me eyes for what matters most. Help me want what You've promised."

One practice that helps me hold onto hope is creating a list of "heavenly hopes." Not just far-off dreams, but things I look forward to: freedom from pain, seeing loved ones again, never having to say goodbye, laughter echoing in a place where sorrow doesn't reach. Sometimes, I'll find an old hymnbook and let the words of songs like "When We All Get to Heaven" wash over me. Singing about reunion, joy, and a home with no end puts aches and limitations in perspective. It reminds me that every step toward eternity is guided by God's hand.

Visualizing a "heavenly reunion" can be powerful too. I'll close my eyes and picture those I miss gathered around a table—mothers, fathers, siblings, friends lost too soon—whole and laughing together again. The comfort comes not just from wishful thinking but from believing Christ's promise that nothing will separate us from His love (Romans 8:38-39). On days when grief stings, I revisit those scenes in prayer and let them fill the empty spaces with hope.

I've known people who approached aging—and even death—with remarkable peace. One friend surprised her entire family by planning her memorial service as a worship celebration—she picked her favorite hymns, wrote out prayers she wanted spoken over her, and even chose Bible verses she wanted read aloud. She told me she wanted her passing to be marked by gratitude for God's faithfulness rather than fear of the unknown. Her courage made us all less afraid.

Another neighbor started a "heaven study" group at church. Every Tuesday afternoon, a handful of us gathered to read scripture about eternity and discuss questions we rarely voiced elsewhere—what will it be like, what are we hoping for, how do we live well now with heaven in mind? Those sessions were full of laughter and sometimes tears, yet always ended with deep reassurance.

Living with eternity in view doesn't mean ignoring the realities of aging. It means letting each day be colored by anticipation—knowing that aches pass, losses will be mended, and there is more ahead than behind. Writing down your own "heavenly hopes," praying for peace about what's next, or even singing an old hymn about homecoming can plant courage where worry once grew. When doubts or fears press close, remember that God's promise stands firm: there is no expiration date on His love or His plans for us.

Small Celebrations—Marking Milestones with Gratitude

Some days, it's the little victories that lift your spirit most. Maybe you've walked farther than you expected after an illness, or managed to fix a leaky tap without calling for help. We tend to overlook these moments, especially when life keeps rolling on, but I've learned there's power in pausing to mark them. Celebrating milestones, big or small, is more than throwing a party—it's a way to recognize God's steady hand guiding you through. Anniversaries, a year since surgery, the day you finally felt at home in a new community, or even reaching a spiritual breakthrough after months of wrestling—these all deserve acknowledgment. Each one tells a story of faithfulness and quiet courage.

I remember after recovering from a tough bout of pneumonia, my family surprised me with a simple "praise tea." We set out mismatched mugs, brewed strong tea, and shared stories of prayers answered—some recent, some from years before. It wasn't about fanfare. It was about gratitude. That afternoon, I realized how healing it is to gather and give thanks, even for things others might find ordinary. You don't have to wait for birthdays or golden anniversaries. Why not celebrate the anniversary of joining your church family? Or the day you first led a prayer group? Every milestone can become a marker of God's goodness.

There are so many creative ways to make these celebrations meaningful. One friend of mine started a "monthly gratitude dinner." She invited neighbors and church friends once a month, asking everyone to bring a dish and one story of something good from that month, no matter how small. Laughter and stories filled her kitchen. Over time, those dinners became a lifeline for folks who might have felt overlooked or alone. Another retiree I know created a milestone scrapbook—not just with photos, but ticket stubs from grandkids' concerts, prayer cards, and scribbled notes about answered prayers. Flipping through those pages when spirits lag brings back wave after wave of gratitude.

Planting something can be powerfully symbolic as well. After my brother recovered from heart surgery, he and his wife planted a dogwood tree in their backyard. Each spring when the blossoms appear, they remember that hard season—and how far they've come since. Maybe you plant daffodils after a tough winter or start a rose bush to mark twenty years in your home. These living reminders keep hope blooming long after the celebration ends.

Shared meals hold a special place in our memories. After my friend Frida finished her last round of treatment for cancer, she invited her closest friends for supper. She set the table with her best dishes, not because she needed to impress anyone, but because she wanted that evening to feel sacred. Before eating, she read aloud a prayer of thanks she'd written herself—naming each person present and remembering those who had prayed for her along the way. There wasn't a dry eye at the table by the time she finished.

Including prayer in celebrations transforms them into moments of worship rather than just social gatherings. Writing down a prayer of thanks to share with guests can set the tone for any event—whether it's an anniversary dinner or just coffee with a friend after a hard season. Sometimes we sing together—maybe a favorite hymn like "Great Is Thy Faithfulness" at a birthday or "How Great Thou Art" on the day we moved into our retirement cottage. Music has a way of drawing people together and lifting hearts.

If you want to keep gratitude front and center, try keeping a gratitude jar on your kitchen table. Each time something good happens—a visit from family, encouraging news from the doctor, an unexpected act of kindness—write it on a scrap of paper and drop it in the jar. When you need encouragement, read through those notes. It's amazing how quickly they add up.

One retiree I know started marking each spiritual breakthrough with a small celebration—a candlelit dinner for two after reconciling with a sibling, or baking cookies for neighbors after completing a difficult Bible study. She says these little celebrations became stepping stones, reminding her that God walks with her through every twist and turn.

Marking milestones doesn't mean ignoring hardship or pretending everything is easy. It's about pausing to notice progress, honoring the effort it took to get there, and inviting others to witness the goodness that carried you. Even when circumstances are hard, choosing to celebrate keeps bitterness at bay and opens your heart to joy again.

Living as a Light—Everyday Acts of Hope in Your Golden Years

"Let your light shine before others, that they may see your good deeds and glorify your Father in heaven."
— *Matthew 5:16 (NIV)*

There was a time I believed that influence was tied to position—to what I did for a living, the places I went, the people I led. But now, in this season of slower mornings and quieter days, I've discovered something deeper: my light doesn't depend on my pace or platform. It depends on Christ shining through me.

Matthew 5:16 reminds me that even the smallest acts—a kind word, a prayer, a listening ear—can carry His light into someone else's darkness. I may not have the energy I once had, but I have a heart full of stories, a lifetime of faith, and a desire to glorify God with what I still can do. These golden years aren't a fading light. They are a soft and steady glow, pointing others to the One who never grows dim. And that, to me, is a beautiful purpose.

There's something remarkable about the small things you do every day, even if they seem trivial at first glance. I've noticed how much a simple smile can lift someone's spirits. When I'm out and about—maybe picking up groceries or checking the mail—I make it a point to greet folks with warmth. Even a gentle "hello" or a few kind words can transform someone's day, and you never know how much hope that small gesture might offer. I remember catching the eye of a tired cashier once, and just by asking how her day was going, her face brightened. She shared that it had been a hard week, and my words made her feel seen. You don't need grand speeches or big plans to shine God's light; sometimes the most ordinary interactions become holy ground.

You can be intentional about spreading hope, no matter your circumstances. Start by keeping an eye out for someone who could use encouragement—a neighbor walking their dog alone, or a stranger in the waiting room who looks anxious. Offer a wave or a simple compliment. At home, you might slip an uplifting note into a library book before returning it, or leave a card in a neighbor's mailbox. These acts don't take much time, but they linger long after you walk away. I've started praying quietly for people I see during daily walks; sometimes it's as simple as asking God to give them peace or comfort that day. If you're comfortable with technology, share an inspiring article or devotional on social media—it may reach someone you didn't expect.

Serving as a light doesn't require a stage or audience. It happens in living rooms and sidewalks, through emails and whispered prayers. I once heard about a woman at church who became known as the "sunshine caller." She made one phone call each morning to someone she thought might be lonely or discouraged. Over time, those calls became lifelines for folks who otherwise felt forgotten. She never set out to create a ministry; she just followed the nudge to reach out. Another friend made it her goal to send one encouraging email or card every week. She'd jot down scripture, a cheerful anecdote, or simply let someone know she was thinking of them. Before long, her notes were passed around among friends and family, bringing smiles to people she'd never even met.

Sometimes the easiest way to keep hope alive is to track it. Try keeping a "hope journal"—write down one way you saw God work through you each day, no matter how small it seemed at the time. Maybe you listened patiently to a neighbor's story, or maybe you noticed someone struggling and offered a prayer on their behalf. Over time, these pages become proof that your days matter and that your efforts ripple out in ways you can't always see. Set yourself a gentle challenge: one act of encouragement each day. Some days it will come naturally, other days you might have to look for an opportunity—but that's part of living with intention.

What stands out is how these acts add up. I met a retiree whose daily emails became such a blessing that her church asked if she'd share them with the whole congregation. Another fellow, quiet by nature, found his rhythm in dropping off handwritten notes around his senior community—he called them "pocket prayers." Residents began looking forward to these surprises, taping them above their beds or sharing them with friends during tough weeks. These weren't grand gestures; they were seeds of hope planted in the soil of everyday life.

You might worry that what you do doesn't amount to much—that only big ministries or loud voices make an impact. That simply isn't true. A quiet faith-filled presence carries more weight than you realize. The world is hungry for kindness and encouragement, especially now. When you spread hope in small ways, you're not only brightening someone else's path—you're also strengthening your own faith.

Living as a light is less about what you do and more about who you are willing to be each day: available, attentive, and open to God's prompting. Even when your energy is low or your own heart feels heavy, offering hope to another creates new possibilities for joy and connection. And there's beauty in knowing that age only adds depth to the hope you pass along—you've seen both storms and sunrises, and you have wisdom worth sharing.

As we close this chapter, remember: every act of hope—no matter how quiet—is noticed by God and needed by those around you. Living with meaning, joy, and hope isn't about having perfect days but about showing up with love in the ordinary ones. The next chapter invites you to consider how your life continues to offer blessing and purpose, even as seasons shift. Keep shining—you are needed now more than ever.

Conclusion

If you've made it this far, I want to pause and say—thank you. Thank you for letting me sit with you, story by story, through these pages. I wish we could share a mug of coffee and swap tales about all the surprises and questions that come with retirement. Maybe someday we will. For now, I hope you feel the warmth of Christ's presence, and maybe a gentle nudge of hope, as you close this book.

Retirement isn't just the closing of a long chapter. It's a holy invitation, a fresh beginning with Jesus as your faithful companion. The world might try to tell you your best days are behind you, but that's not how God sees it. With Him, every season—yes, even this one—is drenched in purpose and possibility. Your life, your wisdom, your faith—they matter, maybe now more than ever.

Throughout these pages, we've walked together through the ups and downs of this new season. We started where many of us do: staring at the silence after the alarm clock stops ringing, wondering who we are without a job title pinned to our chest. We talked about trading old labels for our true identity in Christ—beloved, chosen, called. Then we got practical, building spiritual rhythms that fit the real contours of our days. Whether it's a morning "quiet time" with coffee and Scripture, or whispered prayer during sleepless nights, you've seen how even small habits can deepen your walk with God.

We dared to dream about new ways to serve and bless others, even if our bodies or energy don't always cooperate. Maybe you've found yourself writing cards, making phone calls, or praying for your church family from your favorite chair. Maybe you've started sharing your faith story, or simply showing up with a smile. We didn't skip the hard things. We faced loneliness, grief, and loss head-on, holding space for honest lament and for the hope that God still heals broken hearts.

We talked about the changes that come with aging—aches, doctor visits, and the humbling need to let others help. Yet, we also saw that these challenges don't shrink our worth or our calling. In fact, they can bring us closer to the heart of Jesus, who knows suffering and walks with us through every valley. We explored how to face fear, anxiety, and spiritual doubt, not with shame, but with honesty—naming our worries, holding them up to God's promises, and letting faith grow even in the dark.

We remembered the gift of family, whether by blood or by heart. Passing down stories, praying blessings over our children and grandchildren, and tending to the legacy we'll leave—these are ways to let faith ripple out for generations to come. And finally, we learned to look for joy in the ordinary: a sunrise, a shared meal, a kind word, a quiet Sabbath afternoon. This season is full of quiet miracles if we have eyes to see.

If you take away nothing else, let it be this: you are still called, still loved, still needed. You can find your true self in Christ, craft daily practices that keep you anchored, and serve in ways that fit your strengths. You can name your grief and pain to God, and you can let others help you without shame. You can face your fears, doubts, and questions with courage, knowing that God is gentle with those who seek Him. You can nurture family faith, bless others, and find joy and gratitude in moments both big and small.

Maybe you've tried a few of the ideas from these chapters. Maybe you've underlined a sentence or scribbled a prayer. That's a start. I want to challenge you—gently, but clearly—to put at least one new practice into action this week. Maybe it's starting a gratitude list, making a phone call to encourage someone, or carving out ten minutes for quiet prayer. Small steps can open big doors. Don't wait for the perfect moment. God meets you right where you are, even in the mess and the in-between.

Take a moment to reflect on the legacy you want to leave. Who could you bless with a story from your faith journey? Is there a grandchild, a neighbor, or a friend who needs to hear about God's faithfulness in your life? Could you write a note, record a short message, or start a new family tradition? Don't underestimate your impact. Your story, your prayers, your presence—they matter more than you know.

Before we part ways, I want to offer a prayer for you:

Lord Jesus,
Thank You for walking with my friend through every season—through work, through loss, through laughter and tears, and now through retirement. Fill their days with Your peace. Remind them of their purpose, even when life feels quiet or uncertain. Give them courage to keep growing, loving, and serving. Surround them with people who see their worth. Renew their

strength when they are weary, and bring joy in unexpected places. May their life shine with hope and kindness, blessing family, friends, and strangers alike. Guide them, Lord, into the fullness of this season. Amen.

Thank you, truly, for allowing me to share in your journey. I'm walking this road too, stumbling at times, but always grateful for the grace that carries me—and you—forward. You're not alone. Jesus is beside us, every step, in every new morning.

If you're looking for more support, let me point you to a few next steps. Consider picking up a devotional written for seniors—Guideposts and Our Daily Bread have wonderful options. Join a Bible study at your church or online (many churches offer phone or Zoom groups for retirees now). Visit faith communities like

SeniorLivingMinistries.org or the "Retire With Jesus" online group for encouragement and prayer. And if you want to stay in touch with me or other readers, check the resources at the back of this book. We're better together.

So here's my last bit of encouragement: step into this new chapter with open hands and a hopeful heart. Take Jesus with you into the ordinary moments and the extraordinary ones. Let your days be shaped by gratitude, purpose, and joy. The road ahead is full of beauty—even the bends and bumps are places where God's love can be found. Live abundantly, friend. This is your sacred season, and Christ is right beside you, always.

"Now may the God of hope fill you with all joy and peace as you trust in him, so that you may overflow with hope by the power of the Holy Spirit."

— *Romans 15:13 (NIV)*

References

- *Zondervan. (2011). Holy Bible: New International Version. Zondervan. (Original work published 1978)*
- *Discover Fresh, God-given Purpose in Retirement*
  https://faithinlaterlife.org/discover-fresh-god-given-purpose-in-retirement/
- *Finding Identity Beyond Your Job*
  https://www.ibelieve.com/career-calling/finding-identity-beyond-your-job.html
- *Tips for Creating a Spiritual Routine That Supports Faith ...*
  https://www.bethesdagardensloveland.com/blog/tips-for-creating-a-spiritual-routine-that-supports-faith-growth-in-retirement
- *Getting Past Guilt: Overcoming Barriers to Feeling Forgiven*
  https://insight.org/resources/article-library/individual/getting-past-guilt-o

vercoming-barriers-to-feeling-forgive
n
- *Tips for Establishing a Devotional Habit in Retirement*
https://www.bethesdaseniorliving.co
m/blog/morning-quiet-time-tips-for-
establishing-a-devotional-habit-in-re
tirement
- *Good Gifts Prayer Walk*
https://heidigoehmann.com/articles/
good-gifts-prayer-walk
- *Scripture Journaling—Tips and Benefits*
https://www.familysearch.org/en/blo
g/scripture-journaling-tips
- *10 Best Christian Podcasts for Seniors*
https://www.autumnviewgardenselli
sville.com/blog/10-best-christian-po
dcasts-for-seniors
- *A Guide to Intercessory Prayer | Disciplepedia*
https://www.disciplepedia.org/praye
r-intercession/a-guide-to-intercessor
y-prayer/

- *48 Older Adult Ministry Ideas*
  https://www.umcdiscipleship.org/res
  ources/48-older-adult-ministry-ideas
- *How to Start a Small Group Bible
  Study in 9 Easy Steps*
  https://www.lifeway.com/articles/mi
  nistry-a-small-group-bible-study-pla
  n
- *Testimonies — Christian Mentors
  Network*
  https://www.christianmentorsnetwo
  rk.org/success-stories
- *Biblical Wisdom for Overcoming
  Loneliness in Your Golden ...*
  https://www.crosswalk.com/faith/se
  niors/biblical-wisdom-for-overcomin
  g-loneliness-in-your-golden-years.ht
  ml
- *Lament*
  https://www.rhythmsoftheway.org/la
  ment
- *GriefShare: Need Help Dealing with
  Grief?* https://www.griefshare.org/
- *Leaving a Legacy of Love: Creating a
  Spiritual Legacy {Part 2}*
  https://women.pcacdm.org/leaving-a

-legacy-of-love-creating-a-spiritual-le
gacy-part-2/
- *12 Bible Characters Who Did Great
  Things for God in Their ...*
  https://www.crosswalk.com/faith/bib
  le-study/bible-characters-who-did-gr
  eat-things-for-god-in-their-old-age.ht
  ml
- *Adapting Spiritual Practices to Fit
  Physical Limitations*
  https://faithlead.org/blog/adapting-s
  piritual-practices-to-fit-physical-limit
  ations/
- *Prayers for Healing*
  https://www.xavier.edu/jesuitresour
  ce/online-resources/prayer-index/pr
  ayers-for-healing
- *3 Ways to Engage the Homebound in
  Church Life*
  https://research.lifeway.com/2018/1
  2/06/3-ways-to-engage-the-homebo
  und-in-church-life
- *Fear Not: 15 Bible Verses About
  Overcoming Fear*
  https://info.thecrossingchurch.com/

blog/fear-not-15-bible-verses-about-overcoming-fear
- *Live Out Your Retirement Years With Purpose and Joy*
  https://abide.com/blog/live-out-your-retirement-years-with-purpose-and-joy/
- *5 Steps for Persevering Through a Spiritual Dry Spell*
  https://www.glennamarshall.com/5stepsdryspell/
- *How to Overcome Doubt: 4 Lessons from Thomas*
  https://www.christchurchmemphis.org/stories/how-to-overcome-doubt
- *Who Were Lois and Eunice in the Bible? What We Can Learn ...*
  https://www.biblestudytools.com/bible-study/topical-studies/who-were-lois-and-eunice-and-how-do-they-encourage-todays-christian-moms.html#:~:text=%E2%80%9CI%20am%20reminded%20of%20your,pass%20this%20down%20to%20Timothy.
- *Family Faith Formation Resources | Grandparents*

https://network.crcna.org/topic/spiritual-formation/faith-nurture/family-faith-formation-resources-grandparents

- *Speaking Words of Blessing to Our Kids | Parent Blog* https://kidscorner.net/parent-blog/speaking-words-of-blessing-to-our-kids

- *6 Principles for Sharing Your Testimony* https://www.thegospelcoalition.org/article/sharing-your-testimony/

- *Christian Meditation Techniques for Peaceful Aging* https://www.autumnviewgardensellisville.com/blog/christian-meditation-techniques-for-peaceful-aging

- *Ministry Magazine | Biblical perspectives on retirement:* https://www.ministrymagazine.org/archive/2024/04/Biblical-perspectives-on-retirement

- *Finding Joy Again After Loss* https://www.jesuscalling.com/blog/finding-joy-again-after-loss/

- *Celebrating the Milestones of the Third Third of Life*
  https://network.crcna.org/topic/spiritual-formation/faith-nurture/celebrating-milestones-third-third-life